Heart on a Sleeve

Heart on a Sleeve

❧

Mark Lamb

Copyright © by Mark Lamb, 2015-2016. All rights reserved.

ISBN: 1535026138
ISBN 13: 9781535026130

Winter Moon, Birch Lake image courtesy William "Buzz" Rasmussen. Copyright © 2015. All rights reserved.

Cover design by Ali Pfenninger for Caribou Road, Ltd.

This book was published with support from Black Squirrel, Ltd.
First Edition, 2016

This is a work of fiction. Names, characters, places and incidents either are the product of the author's imagination or are used fictitiously, and any resemblance to actual persons, living or dead, businesses, companies, events, or locales is entirely coincidental.

For Dave

Introduction

IN THIS VOLUME, *Heart On A Sleeve*, Austin-based writer Mark Lamb continues his dive into the sordid, sensitive, and sometimes hopeful deep end of everyday social and family life. A master of riveting psychodramatic portrayal, Lamb focuses his clear-eyed social dissections on the ways that families injure their members internally, especially those with sensitivities that make emotional wounds difficult or impossible to heal.

Lamb's first (2013) collection of short stories, *Do As I Say And Not As I Do*, was a brilliant debut, featuring fiction writing described by this editor in the Introduction as taking us to:

> "...strange, beautiful, and often disturbing places...Lamb's narrative voice is distinct, simultaneously detached and vaguely sympathetic, non-judgmental, but not comforting."

Lamb's distinctive, *sui generis* authorial style impressed itself upon *Kirkus Reviews* as well, who described that initial book as:

> "A collection of seven curiously crafted tales of malevolence and melancholia... Lamb's imagination runs dark, and his stories of haunted lives, repressed memories and sordid pasts creep into the psyche like spiders."

Well: it's safe to say that the spiders keep on crawling in *Heart On A Sleeve*. By offering us a haunting, five-stage novella tracing the multi-generational transmission of alienation, Lamb again permeates the reader's psyche with his shadowy but familiar worlds.

Much of the action takes place in a radius around Louisville, Kentucky (across the Ohio River from Lamb's home town in southern Indiana), as we follow successive members of a pioneering family and their associates across a time period of over three hundred years. Lamb's inherent word-economy, winnowed plotlines, and tight narratives create a happy paradox: a book with a long time-span that is nonetheless a quick read, one that seems ripe with both explicit and hidden layers of possibility and implication. It's the sort of book one re-reads in short order, to soak up more of the tenuous ambience, simmering conflicts, historical oddities, and all the other little details of the lives portrayed that carry big but hazily visible stakes.

Readers experience a familiar pathological family dynamic as it germinates, then metastasizes, over several generations; *experience*, as in *deeply felt*, proving again that Lamb somehow musters our primal identifications with even the most deplorable or off-road of human verities. He knows instinctively that "normal" is a myth, and that all closets are choking full of skeletons. He makes us empathize with some pretty cruddy people, all right; because we know, inside, that but for the grace of God...

We are further treated to a convincing, descriptive evolution of American lifestyle in the area once called (at the time of the first chapter/story) the "Old Northwest." Lamb is a serious history student, and we benefit from his eye for detail in this personalized form of historical fiction, as the lives of the characters (some are actual historical figures, famous and not) are firmly embedded in the broader "life and times." In this, Lamb seems to consistently emphasize in his work how much a product of our circumstances and of dumb luck we all are.

With *Heart On A Sleeve*, Mark Lamb has also developed a unique format. Each of the chapters can actually stand alone nicely as a short story.

Heart on a Sleeve

Read front-to-back, it is a novella, a short novel that carries an inherent organizational logic and temporal and thematic unfolding. The "feel" of it is *noir* - Nelson Algren. There is some seedy stuff going on. But there also is dignity in the most unlikely corners.

Like in *Do As I Say And Not As I Do*, Lamb takes us at times to the edge of magical realism in some stories; and yet, his narrative is matter-of-factly empirical, a "just the facts ma'am" presentation of life in its weirder moments. Who doesn't think they're nuts, see things, hear voices sometimes, believe in ghosts or elves or angels, experience *déjà vu*; who doesn't have carnal ideas about the people in their lives, or want the world to just go away? Perfectly ugly, in a beautiful way, because it's how things are. Like Jerzy Kosinski, Mark Lamb refuses to look away.

We also find that many of the sort-of standard connecting sinews of most "multi-generational" novels are largely absent here, by design. Lamb wants his material to remain streamlined, accessible, lightly obscurant, and yet very hard-hitting. There is no filler here. Hence, an impression is left on the psyche that is quite potent and undeniable.

The reader can and will imagine the intervening and interwoven developmental vignettes, personal betrayals, pairings and couplings, and so forth that might have happened across a three-hundred-plus year period. By loosely connecting his generations of struggling people in a family, Lamb leaves plenty to our imaginations, and this makes for a compelling mental dialectic with a provocative writer. What he doesn't say seems to loom larger than what he does say.

Indeed, Lamb has begun his writing career with a perhaps unintended, yet very wise and writerly stratagem: he always leaves you wanting more.

The Editor

Heart on a Sleeve

I will wear my heart upon my sleeve for daws to peck at; I am not what I am.

– William Shakespeare

Family Tree

Ties That Blind   Richard Collings ———————— Rachel Morris Collings
                              (1777-1840)   (1782-1812)
                              Six Children   John Collings
                              (? - 1812)   (1799-1870)

Heat Lightning   Leto Flournoy (Grandson of John Collings)
                             (1845-1920)

The Earrings   Fern Landis (Granddaughter of Leto Flournoy)
                             (1917-1947)

Give Thanks   Violet Atkins (Granddaughter of Fern Landis)
                             (1963-2053)

Lucid Dreaming Female Descendant of John Collings (Great-
                             Granddaughter of Violet Atkins)
                             (2093-)

Ties That Blind

Each person is his own judge.

- Shawnee

THE SMELL OF dung was so overpowering they covered their noses and mouths with pieces of cloth taken from their mothers' cabinets. Holding long poles and clubs they waited while a black mass swooped and twirled like an angry cyclone in the darkening sky. The clamor, so vociferous the boys felt as if God's own hand was plunging down from heaven to grab them, continued until the mass descended into the trees and spread itself among the branches. Gradually, the harsh noises subsided until all that was heard were the gentle sounds of cooing. The boys moved toward the trees and when they were beneath the branches sagging under the great weight of the pigeons, they poked at the branches with their poles. The sudden ambush panicked the birds and as they flew out of the trees the boys stuck them with the clubs. The pigeons, too numerous to count, fell to the ground with a sickening thud. The squabs, unable to fly, were left behind in their nests. They were the real prize and after the boys had tired of attacking the adult birds, they went after the nestlings. With a precision missing from the wild clubbing they moved from branch to branch, using the poles to topple the squabs and their nests to the ground. Stomping the ones that survived the fall, the boys filled burlap sacks with as many dead pigeons as they could carry, knowing more would be waiting for them when they returned.

The sun was not up but Rachel was, rekindling the glowing embers in the fireplace so she could cook the thick corn dough she had just flattened. It was hot for September and her children slept on the cool dirt floor. John, the eldest, tossed and turned and muttered nonsense. Rachel would wake him soon to eat the hoecakes before he started his chores. She wished there was honey. Perhaps a bit of salt ham would make up for it, though she doubted it; John was stubborn about his routines. No matter, Elias would find the bee trees and bring her some. It was the last thing he promised before leaving. With the fresh kindling, the embers burst into flames. Rachel put the dough on a rock next to the open fire and went to open the wooden shutter to let the smoke escape. She heard pigeons in the trees near the creek stirring and wondered when Richard would come home. It was possible he would never come back. Men died in battle, as easily as she opened a shutter or flattened a piece of corn dough. Whether he was shot dead or walked through the door tomorrow made no difference to her.

The baby woke and started crying. She wanted to be fed but there was no time so Rachel gave her a thimble of whiskey to help her sleep. Sarah looked like Richard when she was agitated. When her face relaxed she looked more like Elias, or so Rachel imagined. The truth was she couldn't tell most of the time who the baby resembled and she prayed it would be the same for Richard when he returned. *If* he returned. She rocked Sarah's cradle until the baby stopped fidgeting and went back to sleep.

A man's voice startled her until she realized it was John, talking in a dream speech that sounded guttural and unnatural.

"Johnny, time to rise," Rachel said. She looked at her sleeping son, small for his age, and wondered if he would live to manhood. The unexpected thought startled her so she brushed it away like a spider in her hair. "Johnny." John opened his eyes, then pulled the quilt over his head. "You need to get up."

"I'm awake, for the love of Jesus!" John shouted, using his father's favorite oath.

Heart on a Sleeve

Rachel pulled the quilt off of John, slapped his bare ass with her hand, and was instantly ashamed of her anger. Instead of apologizing she said, "You're not too old to have me take a switch to you. Now get dressed and pray Jesus didn't hear you."

John went to a corner of the cramped cabin to put on his clothes, tiptoeing around his sleeping brothers and sisters. He hated how his mother woke him, how she would stand over him and stare while telling him things he knew without her having to say it: *Time to rise, Johnny; Cow won't milk itself, Johnny; Morning's a wasting, Johnny.*

He wished his father were here. He knew how to talk to him. *Let's go son* was all it took and John was wide awake, ready to start the day. And he would never hit him, now that John was 13, or shame him. The more John thought about it the madder he got, with the anger burning like a red hot coal inside his gut, and he realized he hated his mother; not just her thoughtless ways with him, but he hated *her*.

Rachel returned to the fire and added a bit of bacon grease to the hoecake. She knew her son disliked her and to get angry with him over a thoughtless oath was foolish. He was 13, not a man yet, though Richard treated him like one. Perhaps that's why John preferred his father. They had never been close: mother and son. He was their first child to survive infancy, after two babies died before their first birthdays. Rachel resisted bonding with the frail boy, born a month early, fearful she would be burying him before he was weaned. When John lived to see his second birthday, Rachel took hope this time would be different. But by then it was too late; she had squandered the chance to connect with her child before she knew she had the chance.

John tried to sneak past his mother. Rachel heard him and turned from the fire to offer her son a hoecake; a peace offering, she hoped.

"I ain't hungry," John said.

"Suit yourself." His words stung and she turned her face back towards the fire. "I'll put some in your knapsack for later." She took a burlap bag hanging on a peg by the fireplace.

"I can do it." John grabbed the bag from her and hastily shoved a couple of the hoecakes into it.

"You want to take Thomas?" Rachel asked. At the age of eight Thomas was the next oldest boy, almost as big as John, with his brother's red hair and freckles but without the contempt John had for anyone who looked at him the wrong way.

"No, he'll just get in my way." John was out the door before Rachel could reply. She put the rest of the dough on the rock to bake, wiped the grease on her apron, and went to wake the other children.

With his father and most of the other men in the settlement joining Old Tippecanoe to fight the Redcoats, there was little field work to do and John's main responsibility was taking care of the livestock. There wasn't much: a couple of hens, an old rooster who attacked you anytime you got close to the hens, a few hogs and a milk cow. He started by feeding the hogs from a bucket of food scraps kept at the side of the cabin. They were the only animals his family penned and he felt sorry for the smelly brutes, rooting through their own shit, unable to roam like the chickens and cow, and finally ending up as a tub of bacon grease. The sun began to rise and he took advantage of the crowing rooster to throw some corn grain at the hens before running off to look for the cow.

Three years earlier, John's grandfather William led his family and relatives to a creek in the southern wilds of the Indiana Territory. They came from their illegal homesteads in Kentucky to squat on Shawnee hunting grounds; interlopers again in a young country which rewarded the brash and the bold, or so his grandfather believed. They cleared the land and built cabins. For the passenger pigeons which blackened the skies and gave them an unending supply of poultry, they named the square mile settlement Pigeon Roost. In the first two years there was an unspoken truce between intruders and hunters. As the settlers worked in their fields Indians might emerge from the forest, occasionally on foot, most often riding their horses, but always, as Uncle Elias was fond of saying, "Close enough to spit on." The encounters were similar: they would watch the whites for a few moments, the same way one watches a beetle crawling across the bark of a tree, and then disappear into the woods. One of the Indians, a young Shawnee called Missilemotaw, sometimes stopped and traded deer meat for a bottle of the corn liquor William made. The exchanges took place deep in the forest where William had a crude distiller, away from the watchful eye of John's grandmother, a devout woman with a hatred of strong drink and a mistrust of any person not born white and Christian. Once he went with his grandfather. The swap was quick and silent until at the end when Missilemotaw surprised John by saying *'til we meet again* and his grandfather responded, *Salanoki*. When Missilemotaw and Elias argued over a fawn the Indian said had been stolen from him, William tried to mediate a settlement between the two men. Missilemotaw would agree to nothing unless the fawn was returned. Elias refused and the Indian never traded with William again. The next year the country was at war and the Shawnee were fighting alongside the Redcoats. After the massacre at Fort Dearborn, William and his sons built a blockhouse six miles north of Pigeon Roost and none of the men in the settlement went to the fields without their guns and dogs.

The milk cow was always wandering off and if something happened to her there would be hell to pay with his mother, who would blame him for losing one of their few possessions. He followed the trail that led from his parent's land through the woods to Uncle Henry's property. The cabins had been built in a single line stretching north and south. Each property was separated by woods that acted as a natural boundary between the homesteads. Most of the settlers were kin to John and before the war he could depend on them to look out for the wandering cow and return her. Now, the women stayed close to their homes and the remaining men had more important concerns.

Henry's cabin was a good mile walk to the east. He headed that way, hoping to find the stupid animal ambling along the creek and chewing on some river oats or wild onions. Cows weren't particular and his fear was she might find some milkweed to eat. In Kentucky a cow got away from John after he fell asleep in the field. By the time he woke up and discovered her, she had eaten enough milkweed to kill three cows. His ma beat him good for that one.

At the creek there was no sign of the cow, but the water tasted good after walking so far. He took a hoecake from his knapsack. It was tough to chew and he regretted not eating one when it was fresh and warm. He spit it out and threw the rest away. There were some pretty rocks laying along the edge of the creek and John took a few of the larger ones to put in his knapsack. They were as smooth and polished as the barrel of a gun and John reckoned them to be as old as the earth itself. His father would know. Richard collected rocks and their cabin was littered with them. He also had pieces of Indian pottery and arrowhead tips, found when the fields were plowed, that Missilemotaw told them were left by his ancestors. Richard would be pleased with the new additions. John took another sip of water and continued his walk to Henry's cabin.

He found his uncle in the fields, pulling flax.

"Johnny boy, come to help?" Henry was short and solid, leathery as an old boot, with a ready smile for family and friends. He was also tightfisted, the easy smile hiding a malcontent who was never satisfied unless he felt he was getting the upper hand. John's father joked that Henry would give you the shirt off his back, if you paid him twice its value.

"Our cow's gone," John said.

"I saw her a few hours ago, in a patch of milkweed." Henry saw the startled look on John's face and added, "I haven't seen her, son"

"Oh."

"How the hell can you lose the only cow you have?" Henry asked, more jovial than accusatory. He owned several cattle.

"I don't know, but I do know my ass is burnt for sure if I don't find her."

"She can't have gone far."

"Far enough that I can't find her."

John wanted his uncle to say he would help him, together they would find the wayward cow, and when they did the family could be whole again.

Henry went back to pulling flax. "You'll find her."

"Regards to my aunt," John said.

Henry stopped his work and stared at John. "Thank ye, I'm sure, but you'll most likely see her before I do. She's gone to visit your Aunt Betsy."

John went north towards Uncle Jeremiah's cabin. Since Richard left to fight the British, his kinfolk had been notably absent from the everyday life of his wife and children. Even Betsy, Rachel's sister, seldom came. Before the war there was always time for visiting and pitching in to help with common chores and the other drudgeries of frontier life. The only ones who came round now were his grandfather and Uncle Elias, who brought honey from the bee trees he hunted with Isaac Coffman. At what point his aunts and uncles stopped coming to the cabin John couldn't remember, but he felt the blood ties were frayed by their absences. He didn't understand the change and when he asked his mother she told him the war was to blame because it interfered with the natural rhythms of their lives. He received this explanation without accepting it and didn't ask her again.

A short distance from Henry's fields was the forest with its vast canopy of trees: The sweet pecan and mockernut hickory, the yellow birch and pawpaw, the chestnut and red maple. Thanks to his grandfather John knew their names and the names of the birds that lived in their branches; and which bushes were of use to people, and which ones would kill you in less time than it took to pick their fruit.

He entered the forest and the bright light of the autumn sky gave way to darkness and the sounds of the woodland creatures, so different from the sounds of chickens and pigs. Their grunts and clacks were like a schoolmaster's dirty fingernails scratching an oily blackboard. The high pitched chirp of a chipmunk, the cry of a mourning dove or whippoorwill were all part of a natural world that made sense to John in a way the noisy discord of the animals and humans outside did not. He loved to be here alone and without a gun. Then, he could enjoy his surroundings, with no need to track and destroy what gave him pleasure. He understood you hunted in order to eat and survive, but he hated it. He especially hated hunting with his cousins, who treated it as a blood sport. It wasn't enough to kill your prey. In their minds you must also celebrate the death of the animal because that made you superior: the master of your environment. John never felt he had any control in this strange land.

It was a mystery to him and he was confused about his role as a trespasser. His cousins didn't question their roles and John never challenged them; he envied their confidence if not their beliefs. Hunting with his grandfather and Missilemotaw was different. Before they fell out, the two men hunted deer together. John sometimes joined them, carrying his father's old flint lock as William and Missilemotaw led the way through the thick foliage. William was a sure shot, his expertise acquired as an 18-year-old fighting in the Revolution, but he was no match for Missilemotaw who could spot a deer and bring it down with his bow and arrow before anyone else drew a bead on it. Afterwards, the Indian would kneel on the ground beside the dead animal, place a hand on it, and mutter what sounded like gibberish to John. It was a prayer to the spirit of the deer, William told John, with enough irony in his voice to let him know he didn't take any stock in such mumbo jumbo. He wondered if his grandfather's mockery had more to do with jealousy of Missilemotaw's hunting skills than with skepticism of a Shawnee custom John thought was beautiful.

The forest gave way to Uncle Jeremiah's fields. John could see his uncle's cabin in the distance and a figure on horseback riding towards him. The horse and rider seemed to be in no hurry and when John ran to them he found Aunt Mary, Henry's wife. She was in the late months of her first pregnancy and the horse, an old spotted mare, struggled under the extra weight.

"Johnny, it's you! Lordy you gave us a fright, rushing that way." John wasn't certain if by "us" she meant the baby or the horse. "Is everything all right?"

"Our cow's gone. Have you seen her?"

"I haven't seen any cows and I'm sure I wouldn't know what she looked like if I did. Here, help me down."

John held on to Mary while she slid off of the horse. She hurried to a small cluster of trees and he turned his back while she squatted on the ground with her dress lifted above her knees and urinated, talking to him the whole time as if they were sitting at the kitchen table having a mug of coffee.

"I thought I was about to pop. It's a good thing you came along when you did. In my condition it's not a simple matter of gettin' off and on that horse." Mary's condition was one she never tired of talking about. The other settlement women, most of whom had six or more children, had little patience with her self-centeredness. It didn't bother John. He figured she had bragging rights to her first born. At 16 Mary was half the age of Henry, who had married her less than a month after his second wife died of the pox. She was not liked by Rachel, but neither were the first two wives.

"Come and sit with me a while before I have to climb on that beast again."

"She can't help it. She's old and worn out," John patted the horse's flank.

"So am I," Mary said. She took hold of his hands.

"I can't," John said and turned his face away from her.

"Yes you can. That silly cow will wait." She pulled him to the ground. They landed awkwardly on their backs with Mary laughing so hard she could not sit up until John helped.

"I can't stay long. Ma won't be pleased if I don't find that dang cow," John said.

"She's hard on you,"

John opened his mouth to defend his mother, but he did not have a ready defense so he said nothing. Instead, he looked away again and watched the horse eating a clump of grass.

"I meant no offense," She said after a while.

"It ain't a good thing to lose your only cow."

Mary swatted at a fly. Sweat dripped from her upper lip and her cotton dress was damp under the arms. Even in the heat and with her belly swollen, John thought she was the prettiest girl he had ever seen. He knew he shouldn't have such thoughts, but she didn't seem like an aunt, certainly not like his others, and she was so close to him in age.

"I must look a fright," Mary said. She took a handkerchief from the top of her dress and wiped her lip.

"No you don't. You look pretty."

"Oh Johnny," she said. "You do make me laugh. I wish you'd come round more." "Why don't you come see us?"

She swatted at the fly, wiped her lip once more, and put the handkerchief back in her dress. "It wouldn't be proper." John was surprised at her answer. He never thought she might think of him the same way. His face reddened.

"I shouldn't have mentioned it, but you did ask," she said.

"I don't mind," John said.

"You're a queer one sometimes."

John smiled. He didn't care what she said, he knew what she thought, and that's what mattered. "Do you have a girl, John? You're a handsome one. I can't believe you don't have a girl."

It was the first time she'd called him "John". He suddenly felt grown up. Without thinking he leaned over and kissed her. She looked like a startled child and it rattled him.

"I'm sorry," he said.

"The apple doesn't fall far from the tree, I guess." Mary brushed her hand across her mouth. "Help me up, please."

He took her hands while she got to her feet. She did not look at him.

"Are you leaving?" John tried to keep his voice from shaking; it was a stupid thing he did. "I can stay a while longer if you want."

"No, Johnny. I think it's time for me to go."

Her slow walk to the horse increased his misery. He wanted to be on his way, but figured it would be unseemly to leave before she did.

On the horse Mary looked at John and smiled. "I'm not angry with *you*."

"I know," he said.

"It's not you I blame." She said.

"I know."

"Do you?"

"Yes," he said.

"You're always welcomed in our home, Johnny."

John stood and watched her ride away. He worried she might tell Henry or his mother about what happened, but he decided that wasn't likely.

The others were right: Aunt Mary was a silly girl who lived only in the moment and once the moment had passed, her memory of it had passed as well.

John passed the blockhouse as the sun dipped further from view. The building stood in the middle of a clearing, like a lonely sentry waiting for orders that might not come. It was a rectangular structure with a door made from heavy timbers that could be barred from the inside. He pushed the door and went in. It took a moment for his eyes to focus in the darkness. There were no windows, only loopholes near the top of the ceiling for the rifles to fire through. The inside was spartan, with benches lining the walls for the settlers to stand on while they shot. So far its efficiency had not been tested. The air was putrid and there was a strong smell of smoke. He followed the smell to the center of the dirt floor and found the remains of a small fire. In the ashes was a blacken deer's skull.

He yelled, thankful no one was there to hear him, before realizing someone might have heard him; whoever did this could be there now, hiding in the shadows. He backed away to the light of the open door and hurried into the woods.

Uncle Elias's cabin was the farthest north of the settlers, the last stop on John's journey. If he did not find the cow here he had nowhere else to go. It was close to dark and he was tired and hungry. He knocked on the door of the cabin. He could hear Aunt Betsy yelling at Samuel. John despised his cousin and enjoyed hearing him berated. A year older, Samuel was big and rash, an oafish bully who took pleasure in tormenting smaller children. John kept his distance and, despite a fondness for his Uncle Elias, he seldom went to their cabin. It wasn't always that way. When he was younger he looked up to his cousin. The summer they moved from Kentucky he worked alongside him as the family chopped down trees and burned brushwood. Samuel could swing an ax as well as any man and Elias treated his son more as an equal than as a child to be ordered about or ignored. When the workday was over Samuel and some of the older boys headed towards the creek for a swim. John ran after him and asked if he could join them. At first Samuel looked peeved, but the annoyed look was replaced with a grin and he told John he could tag along. On the short walk to the creek the boys ignored John. When they undressed on the side of the bank, Samuel suddenly pointed at him and yelled, "Damn, if those ain't the smallest tally wags I've ever seen!" He and the others howled with laughter while John stood silent, mortified, unable to ignore their ridicule, or to strike back. He began to cry and his tears angered Samuel. He grabbed John by the shoulders and hissed, "You tell my ma what I said and I'll beat the hell out of you," before throwing him down. John's only defense was to grab his clothes and run back to the camp. Even then the laughter followed him, like the smell of a shithouse on a hot day. After that, he saw Samuel's self-assurance as nothing other than stupidity powered by brute force. He kept his mouth closed about what happened and Samuel moved on to other targets to shame and ridicule, but John never forgave his cousin.

Aunt Betsy stopped her yelling and opened the door. She nursed the baby Molly while the twins Joseph and Hannah clung to her skirt. Samuel lurked in the background, behind his mother, scowling. There was a red imprint of a hand on his face.

"Johnny. Is everything all right?" Betsy asked.

Betsy and Rachel were the eldest of ten children and the only girls born to a Louisville lawyer and his schoolteacher wife. Their husbands were best friends and when Richard followed his father to Indiana, Elias brought his family as well. Both women were red headed and the mothers of seven children, but the similarities ended there. Rachel was practical and resilient. Betsy was a dreamer and not suited to frontier living; she was happiest in her father's parlor, playing the piano, surrounded by admiring beaux. To find herself a mother to seven obstinate children, in a cabin the size of her father's privy, was more than she had bargained for when she opened her legs to handsome Elias eight years earlier in that same parlor.

"One of our cows is gone," John said.

"Oh," Betsy said, and her casualness irritated John. No wonder his mother thought she was frivolous. "Well, I suppose Samuel could help you look." Behind Betsy, Samuel rolled his eyes.

"No thank ye," John said. "I can manage alone."

"If you don't want our help we won't force the matter," Betsy said, with a harshness that surprised him. "Tell me, have you seen your Uncle Elias? He didn't come home last night and I thought perhaps he stayed with you."

Elias did stay at John's cabin the previous evening. He sometimes did if it was an easier walk after hunting all day. The tone of his aunt's voice made him reluctant to tell her though.

"No ma'am," John said.

She gave John a look that Rachel often gave him when he wasn't truthful. "Are you hungry? Can I give you something to take for the road?"

For a moment John was sorry he lied to his aunt. "No ma'am. I best be on my way." John was hungry, but the longer he stayed the more uncomfortable he felt.

"My best to your ma," Betsy said, as John walked quickly away from her and Samuel and the sorry mess he had made.

When he was in the woods John stopped to rest. It'd never taken him this long to find the cow and his brain was whirling with all the terrible things that could have happened to her. If he headed back now, he might be able to make it to Uncle Jeremiah's before dark. He would spend the night there and leave for home at sunrise. He might find the cow as he retraced his path the next day. He unbuttoned his pants and pulled them down to piss before getting started. A branch cracked and John turned around to see Samuel standing behind him, with a silly grin on his face.

"What do you want?" John asked. He pulled his pants up and buttoned them. "I don't need your help."

"I'm not offering any. Why did you lie to my ma?" Samuel asked.

"I ain't seen your pa," John said.

"Ma knows he stayed there. She just wanted to see what you'd say."

"Leave me alone, Samuel."

"Why do you think none of the family comes round your place anymore," Samuel asked. He still had the silly grin on his face, as if he were about to tell a great joke.

"I don't care," John said.

"You should. My pa's been pokin' your ma."

John wasn't certain he heard correctly. The way Samuel rushed his words it sounded like he said, *My pa's more important than your ma.*

John laughed. "What did you say?"

Samuel pushed John hard with both hands. John fell and the stones tumbled from his knapsack.

"You ignorant little piss-ant. I said my pa's pokin' your ma." This time there was no doubt about Samuel's words and John felt as if Samuel had punched all the breath out of him.

"You're a goddamned liar," John said.

"Your ma ain't nothin' but a slut," Samuel said. He sat on John's chest and straddled him with his long legs. Pinned to the ground, John felt for the stones from his knapsack. The tips of his fingers touched one, but he could not move his hands far enough to reach it. "I reckon that makes you a bastard, seeing as how most sluts don't know who the pappy is."

John screamed, so loud and piercing Samuel tumbled backwards and off of him. John picked up the stone and rushed at Samuel, hitting him square in the forehead. Samuel collapsed and did not move. There was no blood, only a large red mark where John had struck him. He dropped the stone and ran. He did not stop until he was deep in the forest, panting underneath a red maple.

He knew there was something wrong about his mother's relationship with Elias. The smiles they gave one another when they thought no one else was watching, Elias's late night visits, the soft moans in the middle of the night; the tell-tale signs were all there yet John had pushed them to the back of his mind because he could not imagine his mother preferring another man over his father. John hated their betrayal, but he hated the rest of the family as well for not telling him. Richard had left him in charge. He could have dealt with Rachel and Elias if they had told him. Now his family was disgraced, and behind their backs the rest of them were laughing.

At least one of them wouldn't be laughing again.

John wondered how long it would be before Samuel's body was discovered. That is, if he was dead. John felt certain of it; the stone was heavy and he was sure he heard bone cracking. He wondered if he should go back and check, to free himself of any doubt. The knapsack and stones were still there to give him away and, if nothing else, he wanted the stones to give his father.

Richard would be proud of how his eldest handled himself. When he was nine, John witnessed Richard's way of dealing with those who crossed him. The family left Virginia when John was a baby, and settled in Kentucky. Richard filed claim for a hundred acres, and cleared the land alongside Elias and Jeremiah. They planted corn and wheat and pumpkins, raised cattle and hogs, and hunted in the surrounding woods. They chose land with mulberry trees, intending to harvest the silkworms that fed on the mulberry. Ground was tilled using the Carey plough the men imported from Boston at shared cost. Taxes were paid. One day a stranger in a starched shirt and tie came to their home and told Richard the land claim was illegal; it had already been purchased by a speculator, and anyone living there was a squatter with no rights under the law. They had two weeks to leave before the sheriff came to evict them.

Richard would have shot the stranger if Rachel had not intervened. Instead, she persuaded him to go to the courthouse in Bardstown and get the documents he needed to prove he was the owner. It took him four days to reach the courthouse, but only four minutes to be told by another stranger there were no records, and his clearing of the land and his occupancy were insufficient to make legal claim.

The day they left Kentucky, Richard torched the buildings and crops. Any livestock they could not take with them to Indiana he slaughtered, and left the rotting carcasses for the new owner.

In the distance a rifle was fired. The noise brought John out of his daydreaming. He needed to go, but which way, he wasn't clear. Another shot, closer this time. John stood and listened as something ran through the woods in his direction. He crouched low behind the red maple to avoid whatever wounded animal was rushing towards him. He started to call out to the unknown hunter, then thought better of it. As the sounds came closer they did not resemble any animal he recognized. Within seconds a man passed through the dense undergrowth about twenty feet to the left of John, paused for a moment, and then fell forward on a cluster of elderberry plants as heavily as a drunk collapsing onto his bed. John waited to see if the man got up. When there was no movement, he approached the limp figure, uncertain of what had just happened, and wondered if he should be afraid. The man's head was turned away, but he could see it was Uncle Elias, still clutching his rifle and with an arrow in his back. John felt sick and thought he might retch. He knelt, closed his eyes, and tried to steady himself with both hands on the ground.

"Johnny," Elias opened his eyes. He looked weak and his words were slurred. "Help me up."

Elias had fifty pounds or more on the boy, so the best John could manage was to roll him over on one side. Sweat poured down the man's face as he tried to pull himself up, using his rifle as a crutch. John noticed the arrow was lodged in Elias' shoulder blade, not his back. Just as it looked like he was about to succeed, Elias gasped, his hands slid down the barrel of the rifle, and he fell back on the crushed elderberries.

"You've got to warn the others, Johnny."

John said nothing: he was fixated on the shaft of the arrow and where it had entered Elias' shoulder. There was a small circle of blood at the entry point.

"Shawnee…about a dozen…or more…you must go to the blockhouse." The man's breathing sounded like the little puffs of air Richard blew when he was smoking his pipe.

"The blockhouse," John repeated.

"You've got to warn the others." Elias closed his eyes and John could not tell if he had fainted or was dead.

The forest was quiet. John knew a decision must be made quickly before the Indians found him. He wondered if Missilemotaw was with them. It didn't matter; he would kill John just the same. He grabbed the gun, almost losing his balance as he jumped back from the man's still body. The rifle felt solid in the boy's hands, and it gave him the courage he needed for his journey to the blockhouse. Despite Elias's urging, there was not enough time to alert the rest. There was only enough time to save himself.

Rachel gathered her children into the cabin for dinner. It was late in the day and John was not back. She hoped he was staying with kin; it wasn't safe to be out after dark. She had forgotten about the cow until Thomas asked if she thought John had found it. She didn't dwell on the cow or on John for very long because her mind was on Elias. He should be there in the morning with the honey, or not. She didn't care whether he found any bee trees as long as he was in her bed tomorrow. Her face flushed when she imagined him on top of her.

A draft of wind made the flames in the fireplace shudder. Thomas was at the open door.

"What are you doing? Close the door," Rachel said.

"I heard someone," Thomas said.

Rachel walked outside, but only as far as the pig sty. The light was fading and she did not like being outside. She hurried back to the cabin and bolted the door behind her.

"There's no one there," Rachel said.

"It might be Johnny," Thomas said.

Or Elias, Rachel thought, but when she saw the anxious looks on her children's faces she said, "There's no one. Now finish your supper."

When the children were asleep Rachel slipped out of the cabin. The evening was cool. She stood and listened to the wind rustling the trees and the pigeons cooing as they roosted for the night. She thought she could hear someone walking through the woods but their movements were so soft it might have been a prowling animal, or her imagination, or her desire. She hoped it was desire and that Elias was coming to her. She was ready, and impatient to welcome him with open arms.

Heat Lightning

On n'aime que ce qu'on ne posséde pas tout entier.

– Marcel Proust

GEORGE DELANEY SITS at a desk in the back office of his father's store. In front of him is a crumpled piece of paper with a terse message written in a flowery script and signed by Judge L. C. Flournoy. Next to the note is a nearly empty bottle of whiskey. George is drunk, but lucid enough to realize he must act soon to protect his brother from the Olivers. He will not involve his parents; his plan is to resolve the situation quickly and with a minimum of fuss before the gossips have a field day with it. George is slighter than his brother and more thoughtful, less given to start a fight than to talk his way out of one. Perhaps he can talk his brother's way out of this latest misstep. If not, there are friends who can be persuasive.

He tried to warn his brother away from Abbie. She is common, and of low social standing with nothing to recommend her other than soft breasts and hair the color of autumn leaves. There was a time when George thought he was in love with her. Mr. Oliver still worked at their store, before his alcoholism forced George's father to let him go, and Abbie would come each day at noon with a lunch carefully wrapped in cheesecloth for her father to eat. Mr. Oliver never said a word to her, not a thank you or a hello, nothing but a curt nod of his head. He would take the lunch, usually a piece of meat between two loaves of crusty bread and an apple, and eat it silently, standing up while Abbie waited for him to finish so she could take the cheesecloth and leave. It was not an easy trip for the girl. Their house was a good hour walk to the store and in the summer months she would arrive with her dress damp and her face red. George thought her beautiful though, and he also felt shame for a young girl to be used this way by a father who treated her like a packhorse.

That fall he asked her to the county fair. She agreed to go and he picked her up in his horse and buggy on a chilly October evening. The moon was full and George could see how thick and lustrous her hair was in the moonlight. He wanted to touch it and feel its thickness between his fingers, but Abbie sat and stared at the road in front of them and would not look at him or speak.

At the fair she followed him listlessly from booth to booth and took little pleasure from any of the amusements. If he spoke she would answer, but there was never an opening for any real conversation. George soon tired of her and decided to leave after only an hour at the fair. She offered no protest when George said they were going. He gave her a vague excuse about having to work the next morning and feeling more tired than he thought he was earlier. Abbie said nothing, only bobbing her head and looking at him with a vacant expression which angered George.

On the ride home George made no attempt to talk and did not think about her hair or her sad situation. He only thought what a fool he had been to invite such a girl in the first place. When he told his brother about it, Henry smiled and said, "Still waters run deep." It wasn't long after the fair George heard from his friends: Henry had been seen in town with Abbie.

One night George tracked his brother and Abbie to a corn field behind the Oliver's house. An unusual amount of rain had fallen in the summer and the corn stalks were high. Henry and she held hands but did not speak. Instead, the love song of the cicadas filled the silence as they entered the stalks. From a distance George listened as the two lay down, crushing the corn beneath them. For a long while he heard nothing but murmurs and Abbie softly laughing. Then, there was a rhythmic movement among the stalks and George, his silk overcoat so wet it felt like a part of his skin, heard her gasping like a drowning swimmer.

Abbie stands in front of the mirror and brushes the auburn hair that reaches to her waist. It is hard not to stare at the once slender waist, now expanding and slowly revealing her shame. She puts small gold hoops in her ears, pinches her cheeks and stands back to look at the white linen dress with the mother-of-pearl buttons on the bodice. A cameo brooch pinned to the high collar is her only other adornment. She is a skillful seamstress and the dress she made herself, with fabrics carefully chosen from the dry goods store of her future father-in-law. The attic bedroom is humid so she sits by the opened window, fanning herself with the silk fan Henry bought for her in Louisville. The window looks out on her mother's herb garden and, beyond that, the dirt road leading to the house. It is getting late and she expects to see the carriage coming up the hill any moment. Sudden cries startle her and she drops the fan, but it is only the noises of her younger sisters as they chase each other in the yard below. As she reaches to retrieve her fan she hears other sounds, distant yet unmistakable: horse hoofs on the hard ground and the metallic whirling of iron wheels. She leaves the fan on the dusty wooden floor and rushes down the narrow staircase to the parlor. At a screen door that opens onto the front porch, her heart pounding so fiercely she can feel the thumping in her ears, Abbie watches the carriage make its way up the winding road. The sisters, farther down the hill, are watching too, waving as it bumps along. When it comes into view she sees her parents sitting in the front: her mother grim-faced, clasping something on her lap; and her taciturn father, hurrying the horses along. In the back seat, his hand holding the side of the carriage, is another figure: Henry. His expression is unsettled, as if he had just eaten something that did not agree with him. His other hand clutches a bowler hat while the shaking coach twists its way closer to her. Despite the unsettling view of the three disparate shapes, Abbie is elated that one of them is Henry.

When the carriage comes to a halt by the barn, none of the occupants move. Only the horses, two chestnut mares, are still in motion as they lift their front legs and weave their heads from side to side. Abbie cannot see any of this because the barn is hidden from her view. She waits patiently, though she longs to run to Henry and hold him. The two sisters, Vern and Ruby, have no inhibitions and they rush to greet the travelers. Their mother waves them away with the back of her hand.

"Go away now and bring your sister," she says.

The girls retreat without a word to get Abbie. They find her standing on the porch. Her eyes are closed and her face is as smooth as a porcelain plate, but both hands are gripping the rails and the white linen dress is damp under the arms.

"Ma says," The sisters begin at the same time.

"I'm coming," Abbie interrupts. The sisters are not deflated; they are used to being interrupted. When Abbie opens her eyes, Vern and Ruby have already left to tell their mother she is on her way.

Abbie travels the short distance to the barn as if she is walking down the aisle of the Methodist church: head high, hands clutching imaginary flowers, her eyes focused on the man in front of her. At the surrey she waits for Henry to help her in.

"Abbie!" her mother shouts. "What are you doing? Hurry, girl." No one leaves the surrey to help Abbie, least of all Henry. They sit, staring at her, waiting for her to come to them. When Abbie climbs into the seat by Henry, he moves over and looks away at a distant wood. Once she is settled in the surrey her parents also look away. No one speaks while her father touches the rumps of the mares with his whip, scattering the flies, and the carriage jolts back into motion.

Henry knows they have not come to do business in his family's store. He is stacking canned peaches in the storeroom when the Olivers enter through an alley door and surprise him as he kneels by the shelves. His pistol is under the counter by the cash register and he is alone. His brother George is tardy as usual, and the hour too early for regular customers. His only defense is a casual manner.

"Morning, Mr. Oliver. Mrs. Oliver. May I help you?" He knows his nonchalance does not fool them, but it might give him time before his brother or someone else shows up.

"We need you to go with us and right a wrong," Mrs. Oliver says.

"Right a wrong," Mr. Oliver solemnly repeats. They stand above him as he kneels by the canned peaches, reminding Henry of the automatons he saw at the state fair in Louisville one summer. Their weapons are pointed away from Henry. From where he kneels he could grab the barrel of Mr. Oliver's shotgun, but by then Mrs. Oliver will have put a bullet through his brain with her pistol.

Henry stands and holds his hands in front of him, like the stained glass Jesus at St. Anne's showing his wounded palms to a doubting Thomas. The Olivers move back and point their guns at Henry.

"I don't understand," Henry says. Where is his brother?

"What don't you understand?" Mrs. Oliver asks. Her face is doughy, and her massive bosom stretches the thin cotton of her red and white gingham dress. Abbie will look like that in ten years or less. "Abbie is going to have your child and we expect you to do right and marry her."

"Who told you that?" Henry asks, trying to sound offended without offending Mrs. Oliver. "It's a lie. A damned lie."

Mr. Oliver makes an odd sound, like he is clearing phlegm from his throat. "Abbie told us, you sorry son-of- a-bitch."

Henry tries to think of a proper response, but his mind is spinning and he can't come up with anything to say. He looks at the checkered pattern of Mrs. Oliver's dress and feels dizzy, like he might faint, so he grabs on to one of the shelves for support.

Mr. Oliver laughs and nudges him with the barrel of his shotgun. "Mr. Henry Delaney. *Gentleman* Henry Delaney. You ain't so high and mighty now, are you?"

"You can't do this," Henry says. "It's not right. You know it's not."
"Let's go," Mrs. Oliver says, "we're just wasting time."

"For the love of Christ, can I say anything to convince you that you've got this all wrong?" Henry asks.

"No," Mrs. Oliver says, "there's nothing you can say." Henry is allowed to get his bowler hat before they leave.

It is easier than Mrs. Oliver expected: taking Henry Delaney. Having their guns certainly helps; he was never going anywhere without a show of force, despite what her husband thinks. Harve believes reasoning with a man is the best way to convince him to go against his baser instincts. "Appeal to his better angels," he is fond of saying. His wife does not believe any man has better angels, only devils to bargain with.

They have been married for 20 years come August. At 18 Abbie is the oldest girl. Her sisters, Vern and Ruby, are 10 and 11. There was a son, but he was stillborn and the Olivers don't talk about him. Mrs. Oliver was born Agnes Farmer. Farmer was the surname of her mother's family and even though the mother eventually married a man who was not Agnes's father, he never recognized Agnes as his own and refused to give her his name. It is a humiliation that has stayed with her and she will not allow it to stain her eldest daughter's unborn child. Henry can divorce Abbie if that's what he wants, if he marries her first. The Delaneys are Catholic and Harve tells her Henry will not divorce Abbie, no matter what they say. Catholics only do what their Pope tells them and he does not allow divorce, even if the husband is a wastrel and beats his wife and children. Agnes doesn't give a damn about church dogma, papist or otherwise. She is a Methodist and she has her own ideas about what is right and what is wrong and no man of God can convince her otherwise.

They follow Henry out the back of the store to their surrey. As he puts on his hat, Agnes sees what a handsome man he is, with his blue eyes and waxed moustache, and she understands why Abbie would give herself to him. He goes unwillingly, with a great show of protest to his innocence. The more he wails, the more convinced Agnes is of his guilt. The guns are pointed at his back and while this makes her uncomfortable, she knows the threat of violence is wasted without conviction.

Harve Oliver doesn't believe anything good comes from carrying a weapon; men are less likely to be reasonable when holding a gun. At the age of 12 he saw his grandfather shot dead because the old man threatened a neighbor over a missing dog. The dog turned up after a few days and the shooting was ruled justified. A month later, the neighbor's body was found in the woods with a gunshot wound to the head. The coroner said it was self-inflicted, but everyone knew Harve's uncle killed the man. Two lives lost over a foolish misunderstanding made no sense to Harve as a boy, and it makes even less sense to him now.

But he can't say no to his wife. She is everything to him; more than his daughters, more than the son who was born dead. Agnes was a beauty in her youth, with black hair and eyes the color of lavender. It did not matter to him that she was born out of wedlock and his people called her trash. He courted her with a fervor that alarmed his mother and prompted his father to warn him no good could come of such a match. Agnes's parents had no qualms and encouraged the young couple to marry, over the objections of Harve's family. On the day of the wedding the church was filled with her relatives while the groom's side was notable only for the inclusion of an elderly female cousin, twice removed. The newlyweds moved in with the bride's family and Harve never spoke to his parents again. Now, Agnes's figure is plumb and her gait unsteady. The dark hair is sprinkled with white and her hands callused. None of that matters when he hears her laugh, or lays by her in the dark and touches her breasts. In his mind she is still the girl who greeted him at her mother's farmhouse, with a gentle nod of her head and a half-smile that puzzled and aroused him at the same time.

What he does is out of love for Agnes, but it is also out of fear for the hideousness of her anger; an anger so deep it hisses like a poisonous snake and strikes at anyone who challenges it.

They ride in silence, the older couple and the lovers, to the county courthouse in Bardstown. The warm April morning has turned into a hot afternoon, and Henry sweats beneath his bowler hat and double breasted sack coat. He refuses to take either off, fearing what little dignity he has left will evaporate along with the cooler temperatures. His gaze is fixed on the bony back of Mr. Oliver, who drives the surrey in a leisurely manner as if they were out for a pleasant Sunday ride after church. Abbie sits with her head resting on one hand against the side of the surrey while it rumples along dirt roads and cow paths. She faces a cloudless sky, watching from the corner of her eye the shotgun as it jiggles on the footboard between her parents. From time to time Mrs. Oliver turns around and faces Henry and Abbie, holding the pistol on her lap. She doesn't speak but smiles at them, confident she has done the right thing.

Mr. Oliver leaves the carriage on a street behind the courthouse. The guns are not left behind. On the second floor they find the office of the county clerk. At a large walnut desk sits a young man whose diminutive stature is exaggerated by the size of the desk. On its polished surface are stacks of legal books and a name plate with gold letters: *William Wright, Deputy Clerk*. His boyish features add to the impression he is more of a child at play than an adult to be taken seriously.

"May I help you?" The young man's voice is deep and self-assured. If he notices the shotgun and pistol, he has the discretion not to show it.

"We need to see the county clerk," Mrs. Oliver says, "to get a marriage license." "Mr. Wall is at lunch, but I can help you."

Mrs. Oliver hesitates, unsure if the baby faced man in front of her has the necessary authority to help. "No offense, young man, but we'll wait for the clerk."

"It might be a while," the deputy clerk says.

"We don't need to be here all afternoon cooling our heels, Agnes," Mr. Oliver says.

Mrs. Oliver nods her head and Mr. Wright goes to a small alcove at the rear of the office. From a file cabinet he pulls a paper document and takes it to his desk. He looks at Henry, then Abbie. "I'm assuming you're the lucky ones?"

"Yes sir," Abbie says.

"I'd as soon sign my own death warrant as sign that," Henry says.

"That's just what you'll be doing if you don't," Mrs. Oliver replies.

The deputy clerk giggles like a schoolboy who has been shown a picture of a naked woman. "Oh, I'm sure it can't be as bad as all that," he says, and gives a pen to Henry and a wink to Mrs. Oliver.

The sun is about to set when they pull into the side yard of Judge Flournoy's large house. The others wait while Mr. Oliver goes to the front door. He barely notices the marble urns filled with honeysuckle that stand on either side of the door, or the ornate brass plaque that has 𝕱𝖑𝖔𝖚𝖗𝖓𝖔𝖞 inscribed in an Old English script. He knocks and a young colored woman in a maid's livery opens the door.

"Yes, sir?"

"We're here to see Judge Flournoy."

Puzzled, the maid looks past Mr. Oliver to see if anyone else is with him. She sees no one. "I'm sorry sir, the judge is not available."

Mr. Oliver tries to push past the maid only to have the heavy door slammed shut before he can enter. He bangs a fist on the door and yells the judge's name. After a few moments the door opens again. This time a distinguished looking gentleman with dark brown hair and a neatly trimmed moustache stands in the opening.

"Yes? What can I do for you?" The judge is calm, business-like, but he holds a pistol at his side.

"We need you to marry our daughter," Mr. Oliver says.

"It's a little late in the day for that. I'm having my dinner."

"Please sir, we have the license."

The judge walks out onto the porch with Mr. Oliver. In the twilight he sees the carriage sitting in his side yard; the occupants as still as actors in a tableau vivant. "Why the hurry?" he asks, although he knows the answer.

"Our daughter is expecting," Mr. Oliver says.

"And both parties are agreeable to . . . to this marriage?"

"Yes, sir. I told you, we have the license."

Judge Flournoy goes to the carriage. The first person he sees is Mrs. Oliver, sitting in the front seat holding her pistol with a shotgun on the floorboard beside her. He does not know this woman or the man who follows him. Seated in the back are another man and a younger woman, a pretty woman with thick, dark hair that reaches to her waist. The man's face is hidden by his hand. "Are you the folks wanting to get married?"

"Yes," Mrs. Oliver answers.

"I'd like the folks tying the knot to speak up," The judge says.

"Yes sir," Abbie says.

"And you, sir? What have you to say?" the judge asks Henry.

Henry removes his hand from his face. The judge knows this man.

"Henry, is that you?" the judge asks.

Henry bolts from the surrey and runs to Judge Flournoy, kneeling at the judge's feet. "They said they'd kill me if I didn't marry her! You have to help me. Let me stay here with you. Please!"

"Stand up!" the judge snaps. "What is this nonsense?"

Judge Flournoy has known the Delaney family for many years. Mr. and Mrs. Delaney are decent people, despite their Catholic ways. He doesn't know their boys very well, now that they are grown. The gossip he hears is not good.

Henry stands up. "They're forcing this on me," he says. "They said they'd shoot me if I didn't come with them."

Judge Flournoy looks at Mr. Oliver. "And your name, sir?"

"Harve Oliver. This is my wife Agnes and daughter Abbie." The judge does not offer his hand. "We're members of your church."

"I don't recall seeing any of you there before," Judge Flournoy says.

"We're not regular church goers," Mrs. Oliver says.

"Have you forced this young man to come with you?"

"He brought it on himself by shaming our daughter."

Henry shakes his head. "I am not the father."

"You bastard," Mr. Oliver says.

"Now hold on," the judge says. "Whether he's the father or not, this isn't the way to handle it. You can't go around taking the law into your own hands."

"Our daughter says it's him. She's got no reason to lie," Mrs. Oliver says.

"Is this true?" Judge Flournoy asks Abbie.

"Yes sir," Abbie says. She hopes the night covers the shame on her face. She does not want to be married this way. When she was little she imagined herself as one of the brides she had seen at church, walking down the aisle in her mother's wedding gown while people looked on with admiration. Now she wears a hand-made dress because her figure is too bloated to wear the gown, and sits by a man who despises her. Their marriage will be at the end of her parent's guns, not in a church.

Judge Flournoy is silent. Someone is lying and he does not have the patience or the wisdom to play Solomon tonight. "I'm sorry, but I won't marry anyone under these circumstances. My advice to you, Mr. and Mrs. Oliver, is to take your daughter and this young man back and let them work things out for themselves."

"Let's go." Mr. Oliver puts his hand against Henry's back and pushes him into the surrey.

"Wait a minute," Judge Flournoy says, "let Henry stay with me. I'll make certain he gets home."

"You think he's just going to stay at home until things are worked out?" Mrs. Oliver asks.

"You have no right to keep him against his will," the judge says. "You're breaking the law."

Mrs. Oliver points her finger at Henry. "*He* broke the law when he raped our daughter. What's the law got to say about that?" Her voice has an edge of hysteria to it and Judge Flournoy feels the situation will get out of hand if he isn't careful. He steps away from the carriage and watches as it pulls out of his yard and disappears in the darkness.

"Is everything alright, Father?" Judge Flournoy's 16-year-old son is on the front porch.

The Judge is watching the vanishing carriage and does not turn around. "Yes, son, everything is fine. Go tell Mother."

The boy walks to the door.

"Albert."

"Yes, sir?"

"If you have finished your dinner, I need you to deliver a message for me."

The whiskey is gone and George sits staring at the judge's note. He stands, wobbling a bit, with his hands on the desk to steady himself before he can make the short walk to the front of the store. Under the counter by the cash register he finds the pistol, checks to make sure it is loaded, and then leaves the building with the gas lights burning and the front door wide open.

Two weeks after the evening in the cornfield, Abbie came to the store to beg for her father. The elder Delaney had just dismissed Mr. Oliver when he found him in the storeroom on the floor, too drunk to stand. Henry was at home, nursing his own hangover, and George was at the register counting coins. She wore the same dress from the night at the fair and she was sweating, her nipples visible through the wet cloth. She looked surprised to see George and faltered when she greeted him. When he did not respond, Abbie lowered her head and whispered words too faint for George to hear. He knew why she was there and allowed the silence to punish her for choosing his brother over him. When she spoke again, she gazed at George with a frankness that unnerved him.

"It's about my father," she said.

"What about him?" George looked down at the coins and pretended to count.

She hesitated. "His job," she replied.

"That's got nothing to do with me. You need to talk with *my* father."
"Please," she said.

George stopped pretending and looked at Abbie. Her hair was limp and there was a thin line of sweat along her upper lip. She smelled sour, like a barnyard cat, and he was repulsed to think he had been attracted to her. "You need to talk with my father," he slowly repeated, like he was talking to a half-wit, and went back to his coins.

George felt Abbie staring at him and heard her nervous breathing.

"I am sorry if I have offended you in any way, Mr. Delaney . . . George . . . but my father needs this job . . ."

George swept the coins off the counter onto the floor. "What makes you think that I could be hurt by a common slut?"

Abbie stood for a while, looking at the top of George's head. Her breathing slowed and when she walked out of the store her steps were measured, as if she had just completed her morning shopping and was ready to go home.

The men are on horseback, stationed on the other side of the bridge the carriage must pass over on its way back from Judge Flournoy's house. They have been waiting for almost an hour and George's mare is restless, looking back towards her flank and switching her tail.

"Can't you keep that goddamned horse still?"

George ignores the other man and lifts up in his saddle. He reaches for the horse's head and gently pulls it to him until its twitching ear is next to his mouth. He whispers into the horse's ear and then releases her head. The mare is still.

"Goddamn, George, if you boys had controlled that bitch as easily as you did that horse I don't believe we'd be sittin' here right now."

"Shut up, Frank. That big mouth of yours will give us away before my horse does."

Frank Hall is a druggist in town. He's known George and Henry all his life and thinks of them more as brothers than friends. The Delaneys seldom think of him at all except when they need a particular favor. George could have called on any number of cousins to help free his brother: Will or George Henry would have come with him tonight, but they would not be willing participants in any violence where women were concerned. They would not be willing to shed blood.

"I think we've missed them," Frank says.

"We haven't missed them. They'll be here soon enough."

Judge Flournoy wakes and sits up in his bed. For a moment he is disoriented, until he hears his wife snoring beside him. He does not remember the details of the dream, but it has unsettled him enough he can't go back to sleep. He slips on a robe and goes downstairs. In his study he pours a brandy and sips it, surrounded by law books and china bric-a-brac collected by his wife to soften up the leather and heavy mahogany furniture. *The Olivers should never have taken Henry Delaney*, he thinks. He was correct in his decision to write George Delaney and warn him of the danger. Women can't be trusted in such matters and it is clear to Judge Flournoy the Oliver women are trying to take control of this situation. "They can't be allowed to take the law into their own hands," he says out loud. "They have no right to ruin a man's life."

The Earrings

With what price we pay for the glory of motherhood.

– Isadora Duncan

Christmas Eve, 1945

FERN LOOKED UNDER the bed for the missing earring. It was one of a pair of gold crosses Grandmother Beatrice left her. They were the only valuable pieces of jewelry she owned and now one was gone. She was certain she had been wearing both of them when they came to the hotel last night. The man was sleeping so she was careful not to wake him while she bent down and ran her hand along the dusty floorboards. Nothing. There weren't many places to search in the boxy room. The other pieces of furniture, a torn leather chair and a wooden nightstand with a Gideon's Bible, had already been checked. The man moved and Fern backed away from the bed. She did not want to be there when he woke up. She grabbed her purse and coat from the chair, where the man's clothes were neatly folded. The outline of his billfold was visible in a back pocket of the trousers. She took it out, grabbed a couple of dollar bills, and left. Downstairs the same fat man was at the registration counter, drinking a cup of coffee and reading the paper. He didn't look up when she passed him and exited the building.

It was snowing and Fern remembered her hat was still in the room with the sleeping man. He had a hat and she had two of his dollars; something for both of them to remember each other by. The bar was a short walk from the hotel, but in the cold and with a week's worth of snow piled along the sidewalks, it might as well have been in the next town. She pulled the collar of her coat up to keep the wet flakes off of her neck. She expected to see more people out Christmas shopping and thought they were smart to stay in and keep warm, until she remembered it was too early for the stores to be opened. She hurried by Penney's so she wouldn't have to look at the toys in the display window, with the fake Santa Claus who waved one hand, and always had a smile on his face.

Fern was seven when her mother died of diphtheria. Her father sent the little girl to live with his mother on a farm outside Bardstown, Kentucky and then, like a shadow when light falls, disappeared from his daughter's life. Grandmother Beatrice was originally from England. In the industrial towns of the north she made her living as a music hall performer; a euphemism, the gossips said, for a girl who did more entertaining in the dressing rooms than on the stage. At the age of 18 she emigrated to the States and worked her way across the country by taking any job offered: housemaid, bartender, cook, and seamstress; she did a little bit of everything, except entertain. In Kentucky she became the paid companion for the wife of a local judge. When the lady fell ill with breast cancer, Beatrice stayed and nursed her until the end. The judge married Beatrice a few months later. She was 25 and her new husband was 40. She made sure the marriage was successful because life as a vagrant had lost its charms, and Kentucky seemed as good a place as any to settle down.

Fern had no memories of her grandfather, he died before she turned three, but his presence was everywhere in the large house he left Beatrice. From his bedroom with the four-poster he died in to a study filled with leather bound copies of law books and the classics, it was as if he had never left but merely stepped out on the veranda to smoke a cigar. Fern's father was the youngest of three, including two half-brothers from the judge's first marriage. He was also the least responsible and gave up his inheritance for $100 to pay off gambling debts. The judge, it seemed, had grown weary of his constant requests for money.

Fern's childhood was pleasant, if isolated. Her grandmother seldom had visitors or went into town. The highlight of each day was tea time, a ritual from the old country that Beatrice, like her broad Yorkshire accent, never lost. The only other person in the house was Aunt Nancy, a colored woman of indeterminate age who saw to Beatrice's needs. Aunt Nancy was the one who baked the pastries and poured the afternoon tea. She cooked the meals, did the laundry, and dusted the judge's books. If Fern had a scraped knee or lost a doll, Aunt Nancy was the one who gave first aid or searched the rooms for the missing toy. She lived by the railroad tracks in a shack outside of town with her son, Thomas. He had lost an eye in a childhood accident and everyone else called him Bad Eye. To add insult to injury, he was not right in the head, a child in his reasoning and outlook at the age of 30. Bad Eye came to the house to help his mother. Beatrice was disturbed by his presence and pretended he was not there, even as he cleaned her windows and chopped her firewood. Fern was fascinated with his missing eye and begged Bad Eye to show her the opaque muscle that lay behind his eye patch like a white marble hidden in a child's hand. To Beatrice's chagrin he was Fern's favorite playmate. She called him crazy and worse and forbid Fern to go around him. Fern ignored her grandmother and slipped out of the house to follow Bad Eye from one chore to the next while Beatrice napped in her upstairs bedroom. When Beatrice discovered them swimming in the creek one afternoon, it was more than she could stomach. She switched Fern's legs all the way home and told Aunt Nancy that Bad Eye was no longer welcomed at the house. Fern didn't see him again; a month after his ignominious dismissal, he was run over by a train as he walked the tracks home.

 The snow was coming down hard when Fern reached the bar. The drab, brick exterior with the **Charley's Place** sign hanging from the side of the building did not give way to anything less dreary on the inside. It was a dive, but Fern was thankful for the job and to have a roof over their heads. Mertis was sitting at a table near the back with a bottle of beer and an ashtray full of cigarette butts in front of her, playing solitaire. For a woman who would never have her own children, she was good with Fern's boys, a lot better than Fern. Mertis was tall, bulky, a female version of Oliver

Hardy next to the slightly built Fern's Stan Laurel. Her salt and pepper hair was cut so short people often mistook her for a man, which was fine with her; she wanted the world to see her as she saw herself. She lived with her friend Dorothy in an apartment house on Market Street overlooking the river, not far from the shipyards where Dorothy worked the night shift as a welder. Mertis worked when she could and where she could, but her temper kept her from keeping a job for long. She helped Fern in the bar occasionally, though Fern couldn't pay her. On the nights she was there Fern might slip out with a favorite customer, knowing Mertis would stay to close the bar and watch the boys. Mertis didn't mind. It was better than being alone in her apartment while Dorothy was away.

"Where are the boys?" Fern asked.

"Asleep," Mertis said.

"Still?"

"They had a late night. *We* had a late night."

Fern looked at the Falls City Beer clock hanging on a wall. "Jesus. It's only 7:30. I thought it was later." She sat at the table with Mertis and took a drink from the bottle. "Shit it's warm, Mertis. I hope this is the only beer you wasted."

"Not a waste if I drink it," Mertis said. "What happened to your earring?"

"Oh." Fern touched her earlobe and remembered the missing earring. "I don't know." She took off the earring she was still wearing and laid it on the table. "Got any cigarettes left?"

"Nope. Sorry."

Fern got up and walked to the bar. She opened a drawer under the counter, took out a crumpled pack, looked inside and said, "Well, it must be Christmas. I have two left."

"Couldn't tell by looking around this dump. Can't you at least put up a tree?"

"You sound like Dickie and Pumpkin," Fern said. She walked back to the table, lit a cigarette, inhaled, and gave the other one to Mertis.

"Most kids like Christmas trees, Fern." "I'll see what I can do."

"You're running out of time. What about presents? You get anything yet?" "I'm working on it. Goddamit, Mertis, give me a break."

Fern thought she might take a few bucks from the till and hope Charley didn't notice right away. She'd done it before and they'd always been able to come to some sort of agreement, either taking it out of her measly wages or by giving him a freebie. He wasn't an unreasonable man, but the last time she took money he threatened to call the cops and turn her out. Fern didn't think he would do it. Despite the sticky fingers she was a good manager and brought in plenty of business. Still, she was reluctant to take the risk; no owner liked an employee who stole from them. She could use the two dollars she took from the man's wallet. It wasn't enough to get what they wanted, an electric train set, but it should be enough to have a couple of presents for them tomorrow morning. At seven and six Dickie and Pumpkin were very particular about what they expected Santa to bring them this year. The boys' father was no help. On the odd occasion they heard from him, he was the one asking for money; a useless bum, who's work ethic had been polluted by too many Manhattans. Mertis got all of them gifts when she was working. Even when she was out of a job she managed a box of candy canes or chocolates. Most holidays Fern didn't have anything, and convinced herself Dickie and Pumpkin were too young to care whether Santa Claus came or not; the riches of her childhood Christmases with Beatrice were conveniently forgotten. This year was different.

"We want an electric train, Mommy," Dickie said. "Who's we?" Fern asked.

"Pumpkin and me."

"You each expect an electric train?" "No, we'll share one," Pumpkin said.

"Well that's not up to me. It's up to Santa." "Can you tell him?" Dickie asked.

"You don't have to say anything. His elves are watching all the time and they know what children want," Fern said.

"Oh."

"And they also know when you've done bad things, like lying to your mother." Dickie stared at Fern. With his saucer eyes and curly hair, he looked like a blonde version of Little Orphan Annie. "That could be a deal breaker."

"What does that mean?"

"It means he might not bring any presents." "Then we'll ask our dad," Pumpkin said.

"Since when has your dad done shit for us?" Fern asked. "He's never bought a goddamn thing for either one of you, and I don't think he's going to start now just because you want an electric train for Christmas."

Heart on a Sleeve

It was a crummy thing to say, but Pumpkin and Dickie might as well get use to the idea there wouldn't be an electric train. Let their father or the elves take the blame. Fern felt guilty enough.

By the time Mertis left, the snow had stopped. Fern sat and finished off a glass of whiskey while she tried to finalize a plan to buy something for the boys. It wasn't going to be easy, but what was these days? She went upstairs to check on Dickie and Pumpkin. Their living quarters were all in one room: two double beds, a kitchenette, a toilet and sink in a corner. It wasn't much, sometimes the heat didn't work and mice were a problem, but it was home. They moved to the bar when Fern came to work for Charlie at the start of the War. Dickie was two and Pumpkin less than a year. Oliver, their father, left after Pumpkin's birth to shack up with another woman, or to escape the challenges of domestic life (which version you believed depended on who you asked), and Fern needed the job. Oliver wasn't much of a provider before he ditched them and he certainly couldn't be counted on once he was gone.

The boys were sitting on one of the beds eating corn flakes. "Are you in a good or bad mood?" Dickie asked.

"I'm in an okay one," Fern said.

"Aunt Mertis told us if you don't leave Santa Claus a Coca Cola and a pack of smokes he won't leave any presents," Dickie said.

"Did she? Well, Aunt Mertis would know."

"Is that true?" Pumpkin asked. He looked like his father, dark hair and handsome, with a small birthmark on his right cheek. He was born on Halloween and also named Oliver, but when the old man walked out Fern started calling the baby Pumpkin. He was Fern's least favorite of her two sons and she struggled to understand if it was because of the resemblance to his father, or because she just couldn't read him. She counted on Dickie to be predictable, the way a seven-year-old should be. Despite being a year younger Pumpkin was always two steps ahead of her, and it unnerved Fern because she had to be careful what she did or said around him.

"I don't know much about the habits of Santa Claus," Fern said, "but I never heard he was a smoker. I think Aunt Mertis was just pulling your leg."

"Told you," Pumpkin said to Dickie.

"Aunt Mertis wouldn't lie," Dickie said.

"I didn't say she was lying. I said she was teasing. There's a big difference," Fern said, raising her voice. Dickie started to cry. "Goddamit, Dickie, stop your crying. There's nothing to cry about."

Dickie bit his lower lip, a trick his brother taught him to control the tears. "I just don't want to make him mad again," he said.

"Who?" Fern asked.

"Santa," Pumpkin said.

"Oh."

"If you make him mad he won't bring any presents," Dickie said.

"Fine. We'll leave something out," Fern said, "but I still say Aunt Meris was just pulling your leg." Dickie hugged Fern. Pumpkin stood and watched, content to play Doubting Thomas to his brother's Pollyanna.

"It won't matter. We never get any presents," Pumpkin said.

"That's not true. You do get presents, and I'd watch what I say, mister."

"The elves!" Dickie said. He giggled and jumped up and down.

"Candy canes and chocolate bars, not real presents, like a train set," Pumpkin said.

"A lot of kids would be happy to get candy canes and chocolate bars," Fern said.

"You always say that," Pumpkin said.

"You're going to make her mad," Dickie said.

"That's okay. I'm not the one you have to worry about," Fern said. Pumpkin always challenged her, always wanted the last word even if it meant a smack across the face. This time he kept his mouth closed; he didn't want to take any chances with Santa and the elves. "Rinse those bowls and leave them in the sink. I have to go out for a while. I'll be back to open the bar at noon. Don't let anyone in."

"What if it's Aunt Mertis?" Dickie asked.

"Aunt Mertis won't back until tomorrow. Now do what I say."

Downstairs, Fern looked at the cash register. She knew two dollars was not enough. It might buy each of them a toy airplane or car, but nothing as fancy as an electric train set. The least expensive one at Penney's was eight bucks. Pumpkin was right; they didn't get presents that counted as real presents. This year could be different. She needed to make a commitment, step outside of herself and make Christmas Day special for the boys, one they would remember when they were grown and had kids. Charley wasn't going to fire her. She'd repay him, one way or another, like she always did. Fern opened the register, took a ten-dollar bill out, shoved it in her purse, and left.

Grandmother Beatrice's last two years on earth were difficult ones for Fern, Aunt Nancy and, most of all, for Beatrice. At the age of 73 the old lady slipped on the staircase and broke her hip, assigning her to a wheel chair and, in her final year, the four-poster bed her husband had died in 15 years earlier. Around the time Beatrice was confined to bed she started hearing songs from her days on the stage. She would hum along, offended when no one else recognized the tune.

"You don't know what that is? Christ almighty, It's **My Old Man**:

My old man said 'Follow the van,
And don't dilly dally on the way'.
Off went the van wiv me 'ome packed in it,
I followed on wiv me old cock linnet.
But I dillied and dallied, dallied and I dillied
Lost me way and don't know where to roam.'

I used to sing it all the time back in Bradford, not as good as Marie Lloyd, but fair enough. You do know who Marie Lloyd is?"

The songs no one else heard gave way to voices, whispering her name in the middle of the night, or giving stage directions during tea time. In Beatrice's final weeks, she started having hallucinations of the dead. Sometimes she saw Leto with a cigar, standing at the foot of her bed, and she would chide him for smoking in the bedroom. Visions of her parents annoyed Beatrice for some reason and she brushed them off with a curt,

"I'm too tired to visit now." It wasn't long before the hallucinations disturbed her in way they hadn't in the beginning. As death approached, the dead visitors in the bedroom turned from annoying relatives into frightening squatters, unwelcomed harbingers of her final stage exit.

Aunt Nancy made sure Beatrice was kept clean and coiffured, plaiting a dark red love knot into Beatrice's long gray hair every morning. She saw to the woman's needs during the day and sat with her the nights Fern didn't. Fern spent most evenings with Oliver at his apartment in town. He had plenty of cash then, from his job as a sales manager for Jim Beam, and a Model T to take her to all the night clubs that shot up at the end of Prohibition. The nights Fern stayed with her grandmother she sat in an armchair by one of the large windows overlooking the garden, as far from the four-poster bed with its living corpse as she could get and still be in the same room. Beatrice slept most of the time, her eyes fluttering under their onion skin lids, and the gray hair splayed on the pillow like seaweed washed onto white sand. One evening in early December, two days before Beatrice died, Fern woke in her armchair feeling the cold of an old farmhouse without central heating. The fire in the big fireplace was nearly gone so she added more logs and stoked the embers until the wood started to crackle and flames shot through the logs. By the faint light of the kerosene lamp on the nightstand she saw the waxen form of her grandmother, so still she didn't appear to be breathing. Fern walked to the bed. Before she reached it Beatrice suddenly sat up, hissing like a vampire in an old horror film.

"What's he doing in my bedroom?" Beatrice asked.

"Who?"

"That crazy nigger. Bad Eye."

"There's no one but me, Grandmother."

"He's there, in that corner! Get him out of here!" Beatrice was sweating, her lower lip quivering as she pointed to a dark corner of the room.

"I'll tell him to leave, but first you need to lay down." Fern took hold of Beatrice's shoulders and forced her back onto the bed. She pulled the quilts up and kept a hand on Beatrice's shoulder until the old woman was still. "I'll tell him. Just stay put."

With Beatrice watching, Fern walked to the corner. A dark shadow moved in the narrow space. She thought it might be cast from the lamp, but the lamp wasn't in a location to create a shadow in this part of the bedroom. When she looked closer, the shape resembled a human form.

"You need to go home, Bad Eye," Fern said, "Grandmother doesn't want you here." The shadow moved slightly.

"Nobody wants him here. Tell him that, Fern, *nobody* wants him here!" Beatrice yelled.

"Nobody wants you here, Bad Eye. Get on home." Fern closed her eyes and when she opened them, the shadow wasn't there. Her hands were shaking, and she waited a moment to calm herself before she turned to Beatrice and said, "He's gone."

The empty sidewalks Fern walked earlier in the morning were crowded now with shoppers trampling the dirty snow in their boots and Oxfords, jostling each other as they headed to the department stores on Spring Street. The sunny skies, the absence of snow, the last day to shop, all merged serendipitously to fill the stores and the coffers of happy merchants. She hated crowds and shopping, uncomfortably aware her limited funds and plain clothing set her apart from more prosperous buyers. She preferred the dark, smoky confines of the bar to the bright, open spaces of the city.

The waving Santa greeted her when she walked through Penney's doors. Its insipid smile and awkward mechanical movements pretty well summed up what Fern thought about the holiday season. This time she stopped to look at the display window. Santa's clever elves had been busy: dolls that resembled real babies, play stoves and refrigerators, dart games, musical instruments, a wind-up Pluto that rolled over, die-cast cars and trucks; so many toys Fern wondered if there were enough children in the city to play with them. The electric train was there as well, chugging along on a track that weaved around the display window, blowing a whistle each time it passed a miniature train station, and eliciting happy squeals from the children gathered to watch its endless loop.

Fern made her way through the crowds to the toy department on the third floor. A large Christmas tree, topped by an angel that looked more vengeful than triumphant, restricted the flow of shoppers and she had to zig-zag her way to the escalators. The sheen of the glass ornaments and tinsel hanging on its branches was magnified by the store's fluorescent lights. All this brilliance made Fern dizzy; she gripped her purse and concentrated on the backs of the people in front of her as she shuffled through the store. It didn't help that she needed to pee. The restrooms were on the second floor and if she made it before her bladder burst, she'd stop there first.

The colored restroom attendant was busy handing out towels to a young mother in a blue trench coat and her fidgety little girl when Fern hurried passed them on her way to one of the toilet stalls. With any luck the attendant would be occupied with someone else when Fern left and there wouldn't be a need to tip her. On the toilet she thought about what she might do with any money left over after the train set was bought. Mertis and Dorothy would be at the bar in the morning but, despite their friendship of several years, Fern had never gotten them anything for Christmas, and didn't know what to get them now. She was still figuring out what she might buy when she exited the stall, and almost ran into the restroom attendant.

"Beg your pardon, ma'am," the attendant said.

Fern brushed by her and went to the sinks. She set her purse down and glanced around, avoiding eye contact. The mother and her little girl were gone and the restroom was empty of other shoppers. Fern focused on the soap dispenser and let the water run for a few seconds, trying to think of a way she could leave without seeming rude. The attendant was standing next to her and out of the corner of her eye Fern saw the woman was already holding a towel. *What does it matter?* Fern thought. *This is her job. I don't owe her damn dime.* She washed her hands and took the towel from the attendant. The woman smiled and Fern was amazed to see she looked like Aunt Nancy.

"Some last minute shopping, ma'am?"

"Yes," Fern said.

"Well it don't get much later than Christmas Eve."

Aunt Nancy had been dead for years and Fern seldom thought about her.

"No, it doesn't." Fern opened her purse and gave the woman one of the two dollar bills. *What the hell? It's not my money.*

"Thank you, ma'am." If the attendant was surprised at the amount of the tip, she hid it behind the same placid countenance Aunt Nancy showed the world.

Fern smiled. "Merry Christmas."

"Merry Christmas to you," the woman said, before her attention was redirected to a group of noisy teenagers walking in.

The jewelry department was on the second floor. Fern decided to look around before going upstairs. There weren't as many people as on the first floor and she was able to examine the bracelets and necklaces without elbowing her way to the counters. The women working here were older, with bluish gray hair and heavy make-up.

"May I help you?" a saleslady asked. The way she said it sounded like, *Why are you here?*

"Just looking," Fern said, and moved to the other side.

The display case opposite the bracelets and necklaces held rings and earrings. The saleslady on this side seemed friendlier and did not question Fern while she looked. There were so many different pieces of jewelry that it took a while before she saw the gold cross earrings, in a red velvet box.

"How much are these?" Fern asked.

The saleslady took them out. "Aren't they pretty? They're one of our top sellers this time of year. Nine dollars."

At nine dollars Fern assumed they weren't solid gold, but they did look like the pair Beatrice left her.

"Would you like to try them on?"

"How much for just one?"

The saleslady looked at Fern as if she had just asked what day it was. "They aren't sold separately, I'm afraid. We do offer a layaway plan."

"I have a pair like this and I lost one. I don't need both."

"I'm sorry." The saleslady put the box back.

Fern started to say something, but saw it was a waste of time. They would never sell her just one earring. It wasn't the same as in the bar where she could sell a customer any amount of the bottle he wanted to drink. Outside the bar, in the real world, it was all or nothing.

The toy department was chaotic: angry shoppers, rowdy children, crying toddlers, impatient workers; every human emotion on gaudy display, except for joy. Fern tried to find someone to help her, but for every one employee there were at least five customers in need of assistance. Her mind was still on the saleslady who presumed she couldn't afford both of the earrings; who couldn't see the logic of her argument to buy just one. She looked at some die-cast toys. For a couple of bucks, she could buy a dump truck and a car transport ("With three cars included!") and still have nine dollars left to buy the gold crosses. Pumpkin and Dickie would be happy to get anything from Santa. It didn't have to be the electric train. By the time Fern found a salesman to help her, an elderly man with thick glasses, she had decided on the truck and transporter. No one would have to know about the earrings.

A week after her grandmother's funeral, Fern and Oliver went to a lawyer's office in Louisville to hear the reading of Beatrice's will. The office was spacious, but dimly lit and equipped with worn furniture. The windows looked like they hadn't been cleaned in years, augmenting the dark interior. A massive oak desk, covered with folders and papers, stood in the center of the room. The lawyer had known Fern's grandfather. Otherwise, there wasn't much else to recommend the rumpled gentleman with his unruly crop of white hair, dressed in an old-fashioned suit that looked slept in, and smelling of Aqua Velva and bourbon.

Fern's two uncles and their wives sat in a corner, their heads close to each other, speaking in hushed tones as if they were still at Beatrice's memorial service. The youngest, Audie, glanced at Fern and Oliver when they walked in, but hastily turned his attention back to the group. Uncle Albert didn't bother to look up. Three years older than Audie he sat in the middle with authority. He was tall like his brother, with the same ginger hair and drooping moustaches. Fern wasn't offended by their aloofness. Until the funeral she could count on one hand the number of times she had met them; she felt no kinship with these middle-aged men, or their wives.

"So sorry for your loss," the lawyer said, addressing his remarks to Fern and ignoring Oliver. "Beatrice was a delightful lady." She wondered if the lawyer meant that or was just being kind. "Can I get you anything to drink?"

Yes, Fern thought, *I'll have what you're having*. "No thanks," she said.

"Please have a seat and we'll get started." He left them and walked to the oak desk. Fern and Oliver found a sofa, far from the uncles' conspiratorial corner. From one of the folders the lawyer took a stack of papers and walked around the room passing them out: **The Last Will and Testament of Beatrice Flournoy**. "Folks, this is pretty straight forward. With Beatrice's death, all assets from the trust set up by Judge Flournoy are now equally divided between the final beneficiaries, Audie and Albert Flournoy."

"Sorry, honey," Oliver whispered and squeezed Fern's hand. It didn't matter. Thanks to her father, she never expected to get anything from the estate.

"There are, however, a couple of exceptions: one minor and the other a little more unorthodox." Audie and Albert stopped flipping through their copies and looked at the lawyer. "Fern Flournoy gets her grandmother's gold cross earrings and the farmhouse, along with a half-acre of land, goes to Nancy Johnson."

The wives said "What?" at the same time and all the color drained from Audie's face.

"Where the hell does it say that? About the house?" Albert shouted.

"Page five, paragraph three," the lawyer said. Everyone turned their pages. Fern thought it was changing into a splendid scene, much more amusing than she imagined. "I understand you're upset, but this gift is legal and in accordance with your father's wishes. It does not include the contents of the house. They will go to you."

"Cold comfort," Albert said.

"Gift, is that what you call it?" Audie asked. "It's damned thievery."

"It's an obvious forgery and we will contest it," Albert said.

"It is no forgery." the lawyer said.

"Then Father was out of his mind. It doesn't make sense to leave the family home to some nigger servant."

"You can contest it, but please know I am willing to testify your daddy was of sound mind when this was drafted."

Albert stood to leave. The rest of his group stood with him. "That woman will never have our house," he said.

The next morning Fern went to the negro section of town to see Aunt Nancy. Her shack looked like the rest on the dead-end street: shotgun houses that hadn't been painted in years, with boards in some places separating from the studs, and roofs that leaned inwards. The chimneys were crumbling, but smoke still rose from the flues. Aunt Nancy sat on her narrow porch in a rocker, holding an old tomcat who ran off when Fern appeared.

"I don't think that cat likes me," Fern said.

Aunt Nancy laughed. "He don't even like me. He just comes around when he's hungry, kind of like you."

"I meant to come sooner."

"I've got a mess of beans on the stove."

"That sounds good," Fern said. Aunt Nancy started to get up. "Wait a minute. I need to talk with you." She sat on a step, near Aunt Nancy's knees.

"All right. I'm listening."

"I went to a lawyer yesterday, to hear Grandmother's will." Aunt Nancy rocked in the old chair, her face as tranquil as the fixed stare of a marble angel. "The house has been left to you."

"I know."

"You know? How?"

"Your granddaddy promised me."

"Why would he give you the house?"

"It's a long story, or maybe it's a short one I don't want to tell you."

"My uncles will never let you have it. You know that."

"It don't matter what they want. A promise is a promise. I kept my word and now the pigeons have come home to roost."

"You're not making sense," Fern said.

Aunt Nancy clenched her mouth and gazed past Fern to the railroad tracks. The ageless vitality Fern associated with her was gone, replaced by the leathery fatigue of an old woman.

"Why do you think I stayed at that house, all those years? It ain't right to speak ill of the dead, but it weren't for your grandmother I did it," Aunt Nancy said.

"I thought you stayed for me." Fern laughed, to deflect attention from the emotion in her voice.

"Honey, God knows I love you, but I'm not the only colored woman in town who could've taken care of you." Fern shrugged her shoulders and bit her lower lip, afraid she was about to cry. "I stayed for Thomas. It was going to be our home, but we had to keep working there, taking care of your grandmother until she passed. That was my promise and your granddaddy's promise was the house would go to us when they was both gone, if I kept my mouth shut. Funny thing was, everyone already knew."

"Knew what?"

"He was Thomas' daddy, that's all"

Fern thought she heard wrong so she asked again, reminding herself of a doll she once owned that echoed itself: *Are you my Mommy?* "What?"

"He was Thomas' daddy," Aunt Nancy repeated, "and he owed our son *something.*"

Fern sat for a while, the strong smell of beans coming from inside the house and a train whistle blowing in the distance. "Why didn't anyone tell me?"

"Oh, honey," Aunt Nancy said. She looked like she was about to embrace Fern, but she stayed seated, rocking in her chair.

"Did Grandmother know, about Thomas?"

"She did at the end, when your granddaddy went. But I reckon she knew all along. Most folks did. It's kind of hard to keep something like that a secret for long."

"How did this happen?" Fern asked, and instantly regretted it.

"It weren't my choice, if that's what you mean," Aunt Nancy said. "But I loved that boy." She teared up for a moment, but wiped her face. "It don't matter now. He's dead and I don't give a damn about that house. They can burn it to the ground for all I care."

"There's something else. I'm leaving with Oliver for Indiana next week. He has a friend there who's promised him a job, working at the shipyard. It's good money and he wants me to go with him."

"What about his job at the distillery?"

"He lost it."

"How?"

"They fired him. I don't know why. Oliver said he never got along with his supervisor." Fern knew Aunt Nancy didn't buy that for one minute. Oliver's problems with the bottle were popular fodder for the town wags. Giving him a job at a bourbon distillery was the same as giving an arsonist a match and a Molotov cocktail.

"That boy don't deserve you, Fern."

"That's right. I'm a real catch."

"Come inside and eat," Aunt Nancy said. "You won't find beans as good as mine in Indiana."

"I'll be back every summer, just so you can cook for me." Fern looked at Aunt Nancy's uncertain face, one she had looked at all her life without seeing the person behind it. She wondered what her grandfather saw in that face when it was younger, prettier, and less worn by the ravages of a hard life. Had he loved her?

"Come on now."

Fern helped Aunt Nancy out of her rocking chair and they went in the house to eat. It was the last meal they would have together.

Christmas Day, 1945

Mertis and Dorothy came to the bar early on Christmas morning. They were dressed in matching green flannel jackets and dungarees. Each one carried a large bag. Dorothy wore a pair of silver bell earrings that jingled every time she moved her head. Except for the earrings, the women looked like a couple of farmers who had just stumbled in from their fields. It was a cloudy, bitterly cold morning, with over a foot of snow predicted for later in the afternoon. A "record possibility" for Christmas Day the newspapers said, since city forecasts were first started 80 years ago.

"Jesus, is there any heat in this place?" Mertis asked. "It's freezing."

Pumpkin and Dickie were on the floor by a small Christmas tree covered in tinsel, playing with their new toys.

"Look what Santa brought us, Aunt Mertis," Dickie said.

"Oh yeah, that's some truck," Mertis said. She was surprised to see toys and a tree. "It's a car transport, not a truck," Pumpkin said.

"What did you get, Pumpkin?" Dorothy asked. Pumpkin held up the dump truck. "Okay, that's a truck, right?" She laughed and the silver bells tinkled.

"We wanted an electric train."

"Well that's better than a dry hack and cough," Dorothy said.

Dickie cupped his hand and whispered in Mertis's ear. "We didn't leave any cigarettes for Santa."

"He still left you guys some pretty nice presents," Mertis said. "That means you've been better than your mom thinks." She and Dorothy laughed. "Where is your mom?"

"Upstairs sleeping."

"Here's something from your Aunt Mertis and me," Dorothy said. She took a couple of boxes with red bows out of her bag and handed them to the boys. "Merry Christmas."

"I bet it's chocolates or candy canes," Pumpkin said.

"Don't be a smart ass," Mertis said.

Pumpkin and Dickie opened their boxes. Inside were flash lights with a Popeye head that lit up when you pressed a button on the bottom.

"Thanks," Dickie said. He hugged Dorothy. Pumpkin kept pressing the button to watch the Popeye head light up.

Fern walked in, dressed in a terry cloth bath robe and wearing her make-up from the day before. "Who brought the tree?" She looked at Mertis and Dorothy.

"Charley did," Pumpkin said.

"When?"

"I don't remember."

"He said he'd be back today," Dickie said.

"Why?" Fern asked.

Dickie shrugged his shoulders. "Look what Santa brought us, Mommy."

"Are you sure you don't remember what Charley wanted?"

"Nope."

"Anything to worry about?" Mertis asked.

"No," Fern said.

"Good. Now pour us a drink," Mertis said. She and Dorothy put their bags on the counter and sat on a couple of tattered barstools while Fern poured them a shot of whiskey. "You're not joining us?"

"Not now."

Mertis was about to ask Fern "Why the hell not?" when Dorothy lifted her glass and said, "Merry Christmas!" before tossing back the whiskey.

"Merry Christmas," Fern said. "What's in the bags?"

"Dinner, to help soak up the booze," Mertis said. "Merry Christmas!" She finished off her whiskey and wiggled the glass until Fern poured another shot. Dorothy took food out of one of the bags: a canned ham, bean casserole, and a couple of apple pies.

"What's in here?" Fern looked in the other bag. She saw a small box, wrapped in shiny gold paper.

"It's for you," Mertis said.

"Oh shit, Mertis. I didn't get anything for you or Dot." Fern took the box out.

"Open it."

"Mertis found them at the thrift shop on Market," Dorothy said.

Fern unwrapped the paper, taking extra care not to rip it, and folded it neatly. As a teenager she got impatient with Beatrice for doing the same thing.

Inside the box was a pair of gold cross earrings. Fern felt sick, unable to put the earrings on as Mertis and Dorothy sat waiting, expecting her to tell them how thrilled she was. The small space of the bar started to feel tighter.

"You okay?" Mertis asked. "You don't look so hot."

"She needs a drink," Dorothy said.

"I don't know what to say," Fern said.

"Hell, they're just some cheap earrings, Fern, nothing special. But at least now you have two," Mertis said. Fern got a whiskey and sat next to Mertis and Dorothy. After a few shots she felt better and knew what to do: the pair bought at Penney's would be returned and the nine-dollar refund put in the bar till. She could pay most of the money back to Charley, know that the rest was well spent on presents for her kids, and still have the earrings.

Aunt Nancy used to say, "Things work out the way they do for a reason. It's all part of God's plan for us." She was right, Fern thought; there was something bigger than ourselves in the universe, something beyond human understanding, but it was best not knowing what God's plan might be.

Give Thanks

Give thanks for unknown blessings already on their way.

– NATIVE AMERICAN

Leto stared at the computer screen. It was five in the evening and he had been playing *War of Legends* all day until his dad called about coming to get him for Thanksgiving. Leto did not want to go so he told him he was too sick to travel.

"I think it's food poisoning."

"What makes you say that?"

"Jesus, Dad, I can't stop throwing up."

"Could be a virus. There's a lot of that going around now."

"It didn't start until I got back from Papa Kae." Papa Kae was a Thai restaurant his dad liked to eat at when he was in Austin.

"I don't mind having Thanksgiving in Austin. We can eat at the Cracker Barrel or," his dad paused, "at Papa Kae."

His dad didn't believe him. He seldom did, but then Leto seldom told him the truth. The only thing worse than having Thanksgiving at home was having it at the Cracker Barrel with his dad snoring after a few glasses of wine and crashed on an air mattress for the night in Leto's tiny apartment.

"Why won't you listen to me? You're always doing this!" Leto's voice was louder that he had intended, but he did not want to go home. He hated Thanksgiving.

"Why are you yelling?" This was his father's professorial voice. He taught Cinema Studies at a community college and he sounded like he was in the lecture hall, questioning students on why they thought Jerry Lewis was so funny. He seldom gave his opinions directly, preferring to offer them by posing questions that left little doubt about what he thought.

"I gotta go, dad." "Leto."

"I'm sick, ok? I'll call you later. Bye, love you." And Leto hung up. He had not settled the issue for his dad; he would be calling back or showing up unannounced the next morning, but for now Leto could put Thanksgiving out have his head and have a smoke.

He went to the balcony and lit a cigarette. His apartment was on the second floor of a newish building surrounded by older apartment buildings, all built on the side of a hill. In the distance he could see the clear lights of the capital's dome. Even though the city was dominated by office skyscrapers and hotels, the red granite of the old dome was still easy to pick out. The hilly landscape helped. In the flatlands of Dallas or Houston it would be swallowed up. He looked to the north (or what he thought was the north) and pretended he could see through all the glass and steel to the land that passed through Waco and Fort Worth and Oklahoma City to Shawnee, where Sherman was living with Crazy George, the kidnapper. Sherman was the closest thing to a brother he had, even though they had not seen each other or spoken in four years. Sherman was 13, a year younger, when he came as a foster kid to live at Leto's house. On the first night, Leto's dad discovered that Sherman's long black hair, which reached all the way to his waist, was infested with lice. Leto remembered his own case of head lice and could not believe how cool Sherman was about it. When his dad told Sherman it would have to be cut and his head shaved, all Sherman said was, "Let's do it then. How often does a white guy get to scalp an Indian?"

Sherman was an orphan, or at least he was motherless like Leto. The father was an illegal immigrant from El Salvador who disappeared before Sherman's birth. His mother was a full blooded Shawnee who jumped in front of a bus when he was 12. Whether it was from too much alcohol or too many drugs, or whether she was just worn out from her hard life, Sherman never said. He went right into foster care and lived in one other home before ending up with Leto and his dad. He was with them two years, a lifetime when you're 16, until a maternal uncle tracked him down and took him to live in Shawnee, Oklahoma. Leto's dad always referred to the uncle as Crazy George, the kidnapper. As far as Leto could tell the uncle was neither crazy nor a kidnapper, but the dark humor revealed his dad's deep disappointment in not being able to adopt Sherman.

The wind picked up and Leto was cold in his boxers and t-shirt. He took one last drag and then flicked the cigarette over the rail and watched as the glowing tip fluttered in the breeze before hitting the sidewalk. Inside there were two missed calls and one text on his phone, all from his dad. The calls might go on all night so he texted: *I'll call u later.* That should buy him some time until morning. Although he seldom tried, he knew it didn't take much to make his dad happy.

He tried getting back into the game but it was useless. In the old days he could have relied on his roommate, Wyatt, to lift him out of his doldrums. A little grass or one of the many girls Wyatt attracted would have done the trick. Wyatt went to an Austin music school and played his songs in a band with a couple of other boys he and Leto knew from high school. They were best friends, until Leto did something stupid and Wyatt moved out to stay with one of his band mates.

Leto went to Austin to attend the university straight out of high school. In his freshman year he was kicked out for not going to classes. He waited until the Christmas break to tell his dad. By then it was too late to get out of the apartment lease and Ted couldn't do much about it other than tell him he had to get a job. Leto said he would, but he never did and Ted ended up supporting him the rest of the year. When the lease was up he begged his dad to give him another chance. Ted agreed to let him stay in Austin for one more year. Now the year was half over and he was still not in school or working.

He went on Facebook and found his mother's page. She hadn't posted anything since he checked a month ago, except for a picture of her with his half-brother at an amusement park. They were standing in front of a roller coaster. His mother's arm was wrapped so tightly around his brother's neck it looked like she was strangling him. Leto's dad had a similar picture of him with his mother at the same amusement park. It was taken right before she left, when Leto was six. He hoped she would stick around longer for his brother.

Even though he had not seen his mother in ten years, he had strong memories of her. Sometimes he couldn't separate what was happening to her now from past experiences. When he turned 18 his mom posted a message that she would like to connect with him. He replied *yes*, but she never answered.

He looked at the picture a little longer and then typed, *hey mom hope everything is cool with u! Do u think we could get together for thanksgiving? I know it's a little late ha! So i understand if u can't love u!* He hit the post before he had time to think about it. He knew there would not be a response, there never was, but he felt certain that for every change on her Facebook page there was a hidden message, an acknowledgement she was paying attention.

Somewhere in his room he had his mom's cell phone number. Shuffling through unpaid parking tickets and generic letters from the apartment manager, Leto found a folded list of names and phone numbers in his desk drawer. His dad made the list for him so he always had someone to call in case of an emergency. His mom's number was at the bottom. He dialed and the phone went right to voicemail, or rather it went right to a message which said something about the person not having set up a voicemail. He wanted to talk to someone other than his dad. He took a chance and called Wyatt and wasn't surprised when no one answered. At least Wyatt had his voicemail set up: *Hey dude, it's Leto. Just wondering what you're up to.* The boys hadn't spoken since Wyatt moved out in a huff over some pot Leto had taken from his room. In Leto's mind it wasn't a big deal, until Wyatt found out and they got into a furious argument. It didn't help that Leto tried to lie his way out of it, or that it wasn't the first time he had stolen from his friend and been caught. He tried calling his mom again, but hung up after the first ring.

Leto's parents, Ted and Violet, met when Violet was a student in Ted's film study class, *The French New Wave*. She was tiny, less than five feet, with Leto's dark, curly hair, and a tattoo of the goddess Athena on her right shoulder blade. She always sat on the front row, nodding off during most of the films. Ted was annoyed at first; why didn't she just sit in the back? After a few weeks he grew use to it. The other students didn't seem to mind, and Violet was small enough one could have mistaken her for someone's sleeping child. One night during a showing of *Breathless*, Ted glanced over at the front row and was surprised to see her awake, leaning forward in her seat as if she was about to jump into Jean-Paul Belmondo's car. Ted was intrigued and when the movie ended he stopped Violet to speak with her.

"Are you enjoying the films?" Ted asked.

"Not really," Violet said, and saw the disappointed look on his face. "I liked the one tonight. Do you think he forgave her at the end?"

They talked more about the movie and what Ted called the *nouvelle vague*. When she asked him if he wanted to have a drink somewhere he said yes and they ended up in a country bar where Garth Brooks played in the background and no one had heard of Godard or Jean Seberg and thought the French were funny aliens from another planet.

They talked about Ted's childhood on a north Texas chicken farm where the days started at 5:00 in the morning and consisted mostly of cleaning the shit off of your boots and making certain the chickens didn't eat each other. The only comments Violet made about her childhood (she was originally from a small town in Indiana) were vague ones about parents who loved the bottle more than their own children, and about a great-grandfather who had been a well-respected judge in Kentucky.

He wanted to protect her, this grown up child he knew nothing about, and before the semester was over they were living together in Ted's loft overlooking the Port of Houston.

Leto, named after the great-grandfather in Kentucky, was born a year later. Ted immediately cast himself in the dual roles of father and mother, assigning Violet a walk-on part in his vanity production. He was the one who bathed Leto, made sure his clothes matched and were clean, and the boy learned (Ted's version of) right from wrong. He enrolled him in a Montessori school and attended all the parent-teacher conferences alone while Violet stayed home, smoking unfiltered Camels and watching old movies on TCM. Ted felt superior to her in every way and thought his taking charge of their son proved it; he couldn't see that his control was the disease and not the cure.

The only times Violet showed her maternal instincts were in the evenings, before Leto fell asleep. She'd lie next to him in the dark while the lights from the port flickered above them like illuminated specks of fairy dust, and stroke his forehead. Sometimes she recited passages from *When*

Heart on a Sleeve

We Were Very Young. Sometimes she sang *Twinkle, Twinkle Little Star.* Most nights they would curl up side by side, the mother not much larger than her child, and watch the fairy dust float across the ceiling.

She left with a graduate student in engineering when Leto was six. Unlike Ted, the student saw the world in color and did not have time for French movies or fairy dust.

Ted never got over Violet leaving him. He blamed her selfishness, but insisted his anger wouldn't affect Leto's relationship with her. He refused to date, and justified the sacrifice by convincing himself one overachieving parent was better than two in conflict. He moved Leto to a house in the suburbs where they went to Halloween block parties and hosted backyard barbeques on the 4th of July. He arranged playdates with other parents and spent summers coaching Leto's baseball team, despite his antipathy for sports. On weekends they watched movies with subtitles or visited a museum. Every fall they traveled to a national park and camped. But Leto still struggled in school and in his association with other kids. Ted thought self-absorption was the problem, and decided the boy needed a brother to teach him how to care about someone other than himself. He applied to be a foster parent, not realizing he had given up on his son and was now trying to replace him.

Sherman had been in another foster home before he went to live with Ted and Leto. It was run by Miss Margie, a middle aged lady who meant well, but could not control the three younger boys already staying with her when Sherman arrived. Having been together for the past six months the boys operated as a single hostile entity towards anyone new or different and, from the first day Sherman moved in, tormented him. They made fun of his long hair and the two earrings he wore. Behind Miss Margie's back they called him "Tonto". They were sad boys with sad stories, but Sherman's start in life was just as miserable. Instead of retaliation Sherman opted for retreat. Two times he ran away and two times he was brought back. On the third try Sherman stole money from Miss Margie's purse and tried to buy a one-way ticket to Oklahoma City. A young boy buying a one-way ticket was certain to set off alarms. The authorities were called and Sherman was back with Miss Margie again, but not for long; the old woman could put up with a lot from her foster kids, but running away and stealing were two things she would not tolerate. Sherman was placed with Ted and Leto the following week.

Despite Sherman's rough past, he was easy for Ted. He ate whatever was put in front of him and helped out around the house without being asked. He enjoyed cutting grass on the riding lawnmower and grocery shopping. The first year Ted assumed Sherman was going along just to get along, and things would eventually change. They didn't. Sherman was so worn out from the years of living with an alcoholic mother and wondering what the next day would bring, he was grateful for the constancy and smart enough not to invite discord. Sherman could be moody and take himself away for no obvious reason. He was, to Ted's chagrin, a smoker and not interested in art films or art museums, but Ted knew when to back off and leave him alone. He knew how to be an effective parent to a child who was not his, in a way he never managed with Leto.

Leto and Sherman got along from the start. Leto helped his foster brother navigate his new school and in the evenings they did homework together, with Sherman helping Leto survive his first year of algebra. Ted coached them on the same baseball team and for the first time enjoyed it. Sherman was the brother Ted hoped he would be, but it came at a cost. Leto had long ago given up trying to impress his dad, but he did want to impress Sherman and he began to compete with Ted for the boy's attention. Instead of being angry at the usurper stealing his father's approval, Leto was angry at his father for stealing his friend's affection.

One summer, when Leto was 15 and Sherman 14, Ted took them to Big Bend Park in the southwestern part of Texas where the only thing that separates the U. S. from Mexico is the snaky Rio Grande River. Ted called it a camping trip even though he hated camping and had booked a room for them at the Chisos Mountains lodge. The room was small, dated and with a window air unit so loud it was difficult to carry on a conversation when it was running. That was fine with Leto, who hadn't spoken for most of the 12-hour drive. He was angry with his dad for coming up with this lame vacation, angry about being taken from his computer for a week, but mostly he was angry because Sherman had called *Shotgun!* and jumped in the front passenger's seat before the car pulled out of the driveway. Sherman was the only reason Leto agreed to go to Big Bend. He was counting on Sherman to be his co-conspirator so they could laugh behind Ted's back at his tendency to see everything as a teachable moment, to view the world as a giant classroom with him as Peter O'Toole in the pulpy remake of *Goodbye, Mr. Chips* and the boys just along for the ride, enthusiastic extras who were thankful to be basking in reflected glory. A team of two against one is what they would be, Leto thought, more like Malcolm McDowell and his mates from *A Clockwork Orange*, speaking their own language and trashing Ted's world. Now Sherman was a co-conspirator with Ted, sitting in the front seat chatting away, while Leto was left in the back, tossed aside like a crumpled bag of half-eaten chips.

The common areas of the lodge had spectacular views of the mountains; Ted and the boys spent a lot of time there when they weren't exploring. In typical Ted fashion he planned their itinerary without consulting anyone because in his mind he had read enough about Big Bend to separate the best trails from the touristy ones. He never defined "best" and the touristy remark made little sense in a part of the state so remote it felt more like one of Jupiter's moons than a national park. It didn't matter to Sherman. He went along with whatever Ted said, but Leto sulked and shadowed them on every hike; a grim, silent specter, determined to haunt the trip.

They started their days at dawn with breakfast in the lodge before setting out on whatever outing Ted had planned. Traveling on foot or by car, their equipment was the same: 8 ounces of water per hour per person, sunscreen, lip balm, sunglasses, hiking boots, and wide-brimmed hats. Leto refused to wear the hat or hiking boots, choosing instead his baseball cap and Nikes.

One morning Ted got the boys up before daylight. They skipped breakfast at the lodge and packed some granola bars to eat later. Leto and Sherman slept in the back seat while Ted drove for miles on an old mining road through the low desert with the ancient Chisos Mountains silhouetted in the east like a giant cardboard cutout against the hazy sky. When he pulled off the road into a dusty parking area, the sky was turning a misty blue with the shadows of low lying clouds moving rapidly over the landscape.

"Wake up guys. We're here."

"Here" of course did not mean where they were supposed to be. They took their water canteens and the granola bars and hiked a mile until they came to what Ted wanted to show them: the remains of an old ranch house. There wasn't much left standing, other than a few adobe walls and part of the tin roof. Close by a crooked windmill stood as a sentry, still pulling water from the ground after a hundred years. Fruit trees surrounded the house and gave welcomed shade from a day already heating up. But it wasn't just the sights Ted wanted to show them. It was the sounds as well. Dozens of desert song birds, drawn by the spring water and the fig and pecan trees, sang in the early morning light. Sherman recognized a couple of them: the yellow-billed cuckoo and something called Bell's vireo. A few others Ted identified with his guide book. While Ted and Sherman stayed near the old house, Leto took one of the earthen paths and followed it to a grove of walnut trees. On a crude wooden bench at the end of the path, he sat down to listen.

They decided to have lunch in Terlingua, an old mining town by the river. That is, Ted and Sherman decided to have lunch there. Leto wanted to go back to the campgrounds and eat at the lodge. He was hot and tired and for him the day was over.

"It'll be fun. They've converted an old movie theatre into a restaurant and bar," Ted said when they left the parking area and drove toward the road.

"Wow. Impressive. Maybe you can lecture the locals on French cinema," Leto said.

Ted didn't respond. From the front seat Sherman turned around and glared at Leto.

A sign in the entrance to the Terlingua Bar and Grill said, Live Music! Other than a small group of rafters sitting at the bar, the restaurant was empty. The inside was impressive with linen covered tables scattered about a cavernous art deco interior. The boys ordered burgers and fries. Ted ordered a bottle of red wine and a sirloin steak.

"Jesus, Dad. It's lunch, not dinner. Remember, you're the designated driver here."

"I'll be fine. Hey, we're on vacation. Right, Sherman?"

"That's right, Dad," Sherman said.

"*Dad*," Leto mimicked. Sherman had never called Ted that before. It gave Leto a sick feeling in his stomach. When the food came everyone ate in silence. After a second bottle of wine Ted got up from the table, knocking his chair over. Sherman helped to pick it up.

"I'm going to find out when the music starts," Ted said.

"Want me to go with you?" Sherman asked.

"No, Son. I'm fine," Ted said, and he walked to the bar without knocking anything else over.

"Why are you such a dick to Ted?" Sherman asked. There was no rancor in his voice, just curiosity and maybe a little pity.

"You mean to *Dad*?" Leto responded, but the question stung. He didn't see himself that way with Ted.

"You're always so pissed off around him. Show more respect. At least you have a dad"

It frightened Leto to think Sherman cared more for Ted than he did, and for a moment he thought he might cry. He left the table and went outside. He hoped Sherman would follow him, but Sherman stayed behind. He walked to their car and sat on the hood. The mountains were all around, cradling him, and it made Leto think of his mother and the nights she would lay next to him when he was little, before she left. When he closed his eyes he could hear her voice, feel her close to him, and this almost made the fear go away.

The morning Sherman's Uncle George came to get him happened almost two years to the day Child Protective Services placed Sherman with Ted and Leto. It took that long for the agency to locate family members in Oklahoma and then decide which ones were stable enough to take Sherman. George was a police officer in Shawnee and once he passed all the drug and home visit tests, he jumped to the front of the line. The truth was, George was the only one in the family able to do it. There was one other uncle and two aunts, but all of them had too many problems or too many kids. George was single, made a decent salary, and had no responsibilities other than his job. He wanted his sister's son to be raised in Shawnee traditions, surrounded by his clan, and not with some random white family hundreds of miles away.

Ted and Leto helped Sherman pack the night before he left. The slow, methodical way Ted went about gathering Sherman's possessions frustrated the boys, and they convinced him to take a break while they finished. Leto was thankful to have some private time with Sherman. There hadn't been much of that since CPS told them he was going to be placed with his uncle; Ted wouldn't leave the two alone, and insisted on every meal and outing being spent together. Leto understood his dad wanted to adopt Sherman and resented George (who in private he called Crazy George) for suddenly popping up after two years, but Ted's exaggerated response was disturbing to him. What Leto couldn't admit was neither of them wanted to be around each other without Sherman.

George was not what they expected: he was short and muscular, sporting a crew cut, and speaking in a voice so low it was difficult to hear everything he said. He arrived with Sherman's social worker promptly at eight and walked into the house like it was a crime scene he had come to investigate. After the introductions there wasn't much small talk and Ted was surprised when George told Sherman to get his things because they had a long ride back to Oklahoma.

In the front yard Ted and George exchanged addresses and everyone promised to keep in contact, but Leto knew, even if his dad didn't, no one would be calling or staying in touch. Sherman was going to his real home, and his temporary family would have to pick up where they left off.

The waitress at Cracker Barrel took Ted to a table in the middle of the dining room.

"Is anyone else joining you?" the waitress asked. She was a middle aged woman, with a bowl-shaped hair cut who probably had a family waiting for her at home; or maybe she didn't, and had volunteered to take another waitress's shift on Thanksgiving.

"Yes," Ted said, although he doubted Leto would show up.

"Can I get you anything to drink?"

"A glass of wine, please. A Cab."

"Any particular kind?"

"It doesn't matter."

"Yes, sir. My name is Linda if you need anything."

"Thank you."

Linda gave him the same concerned smile his mother use to give him when she knew he was lying, and then left to wait on another table.

Ted was the only person seated alone in the crowded restaurant, like an island surrounded by waves of families. He looked at the menu while a young couple behind him, with a restless toddler and a screaming baby, argued over how much of a tip to leave; and an elderly man on a walker was helped to the next table by a teenaged girl. The girl was attentive to the man and held his arm as he lowered himself onto the chair. Women were the caregivers, that was the conventional wisdom, but Leto's mother left and Ted was the one who took care of his son. *Leto should be taking care of me now*, Ted thought. His life might have been different if Sherman had been his son and Leto the foster child. The universe was supposed to be perfect, but it fucked up all the time: the wrong child placed with the wrong parent and the true son claimed by another. It was like a Grimm fairy tale come to life.

"Are you still waiting or would you like to order now?" Linda was back with his glass of wine.

"I'm still waiting," Ted said, and took a sip of wine.

Leto walked past the governor's mansion on Colorado Street towards Congress Avenue. On Congress he had a better view of the Capital. There weren't many people out on this chilly evening and the surreal sight of the garishly lighted building, with the Goddess of Liberty statue staring at him from the top of the rotunda, made Leto feel he was on a futuristic film set. He lit a cigarette and pulled a rumpled piece of paper from his pocket with an address written in his father's neat lettering. Tomorrow he would buy a ticket to Shawnee to see Sherman. He was certain Sherman and Crazy George would let him stay with them until he figured out what he wanted, away from his father and mother. There was nothing for him here and his dad would have to accept that. Sherman was the only family he'd known and he wanted to be with family; he wanted to believe there was still fairy dust.

He turned from the staring goddess and started walking down the avenue.

Lucid Dreaming

Why should I fear death? If I am, then death is not.

- Epicurus

THE ROOM WAS a brilliant white cube with neither an entrance nor an exit. The only pieces of furniture were in the center: a reclining, red-leather chair and a wooden table with a shiny metal tray on top similar to one you might have found in a dentist's office 100 years ago. A wine goblet sat in the middle of the tray. The woman was nervous but after seeing the bland serenity of the room, she felt comforted and less agitated. The smooth, professional tone of the technician helped.

"Please, have a seat. Would you like to take your shoes off?" The technician was a newer model and very life- like. The woman was tempted to touch the soft face until she realized that would be insensitive. It was hard to tell if it was designed to be a male or a female. Either way there were certain emotions programmed into its data base and while she couldn't be sure embarrassment was one of them, she did not want to risk it.

"Yes, that would be lovely." The woman slipped off her shoes and the technician took them and placed them on the floor. She settled into the soft contours of the chair. "Will this take long?"

The technician looked perplexed, like one of the old time comedians the woman had once seen at the Cinema Revival Theatre. All that was missing was the funny little moustache.

Perhaps the technician hadn't heard her so she spoke slower with a special emphasis on the last word. It was the same technique the woman used with her international students. "Will this take *long*?"

The technician was frozen with the same quizzical expression. The woman felt light headed and the comfort was replaced by a cold panic. She wanted to bolt from the chair until her sensible nature took control and she thought of a rational explanation for the technician's odd response: she needed to be more exact.

"Will the *erasure* take long?"

The curious look vanished and the technician said, "No, not long." The woman relaxed.

"Which music would you prefer?" The technician asked. "Sorry?"

"Which music would you prefer? The memories are most easily activated by music that is particular to them. Or perhaps a special smell? That is equally effective."

The woman hadn't expected this odd request, but it made sense. All the books she'd read on the brain mentioned the strong association between music and memories. It had something to do with familiar music serving as a kind of soundtrack for a mental film. When the person heard the music it activated the hub where long ago memories were stored, turning them into a personal home movie.

There were so many memories and so much music to choose from. "I don't know. Is it really necessary?"

"It's much less painful with some type of stimulus." The technician smiled.

"Painful? I was under the impression there wasn't any pain involved." The woman rubbed her hands.

"I am talking about emotional pain, not physical pain. There isn't any physical pain." The technician was speaking to her now as if she were the student.

"I know what you mean." She sounded peevish and regretted the tone in her voice.

The technician ignored the comment, or perhaps petulance was not an emotion it recognized. "Please, take as long as you need. I'll get the paperwork." And it was gone, leaving the woman alone to consider her decision.

The anti-erasure protesters huddled in the rain outside the massive barriers of the clinic compound, with their furious faces and threatening placards, hadn't helped matters when she approached the entrance. The invisible fences on either side of the road kept them clear of her soundproof vehicle, but they were still a frightening sight as they mouthed obscenities and attacked the air with their signs. Where did so much anger come from? It was easy to dismiss them as a fringe element of society; maybe there was a truth buried beneath the histrionics.

Her husband agreed with them. "It's like killing him again," he said. "The memories will keep him alive for you." He really meant, *for me*. He found solace in the pain and would find a way to get past it, cherishing the boy's memory in the sweet, reverent way peculiar to him. Her husband knew how to mourn. The woman didn't. Her pain was like a parasite eating its way through her gut, something that needed to be cut out. She couldn't focus on anything other than her deceased son and she resented it. The dead had no right to claim the attention of the living. Their relationship had been difficult enough when the son was alive. So much time lost to slammed doors and spiteful words.

When they came home from the remembrance ceremony the only thought the woman had was this: *they would never argue again*. She went into her study and started working on the class lectures that had been put aside after the accident. Her husband stood at the closed doors of the study, staring through the glass panes with his hands pressed against the glass.

The woman's pragmatism gave way to guilt. Guilt that came from realizing she hated her son. Not always, certainly not in the early years when she took pleasure in their museum trips and visits to the Cinema Revival House. Everyone said they had much in common. The woman's friends told her how they envied the connection between mother and son. "I love you very, *very* much," the little boy told her each night before he fell asleep and the woman would softly sing a few lines from *Twinkle, Twinkle, Little Star* before turning out the lights.

Those memories were buried under the mounds of garbage their relationship had accumulated during the teen- age years. It became an impossible feat of sorcery to conjure up those happier times. Now her son was dead and all she had left was the pain of guilt and the certain knowledge nothing could reshape the awful past.

The technician returned with an electronic pad and a pitcher filled with a honey-colored liquid. It placed the pitcher on the metal tray next to the wine goblet and handed the pad to the woman. "Are you ready to get started?" There was a slight smile on the technician's face.

"Yes." There were no other options. Her husband could accept her decision or not. It really didn't matter since there was a strong possibility he would not be waiting when she returned to the house.

"Then if you would sign here and initial this line, please, we'll get under way." The woman signed and handed the electronic pad to the technician who slid it into an over-sized pocket in its lab coat. From another pocket the technician took out a device that looked like a remote control for a media center. The woman noticed a slight fraying along the cuffs of one of the android's coat sleeves. For a moment she felt sorry for the technician. "Have you decided on your music?"

"Yes. *Twinkle, Twinkle, Little Star*," the woman said.

"Lovely," the technician said. "Any particular version?"

"It doesn't matter," she replied.

"Now, this is all very straight forward, nothing to be worried about."

"I'm not worried," the woman said.

The technician poured the honey colored liquid into the goblet. It looked like an expensive cocktail without the paper umbrella. If she closed her eyes she could imagine herself in the bar of a five-star resort instead of being in the sterile cube of an erasure center.

"When you drink this," the technician said, "it will stimulate the areas of the brain where episodic memories are stored. These are memories of autobiographical events. The longer the drug is in your system, the more vivid and extensive the memory recall will be." The technician showed the woman the device that looked like a remote control.

"This will act as an external stimulus to control the selection of your memories. You want to focus on the subject of the erasure and make certain that only those memories are targeted. Otherwise you could inadvertently eliminate another subject. This is not a linear process; the memories will occur randomly. Once the target appears, press this green button and all subsequent memories will be confined to the target. For each memory you then press the red button and it's deleted. When all of the memories have been deleted erasure will occur and the target, at least in memory form, will no longer exist for you. *Click*, delete. It's very simple."

"Will I be aware of what I'm doing?" The woman asked. "I mean, I'll be unconscious, won't I?"

"Semi-conscious, as long as you do not remain in a memory too long. The deeper you go the harder it will be for you to control this process and then . . ." the technician trailed off.

"Yes?"

"Just remember to delete the memory as soon as you enter it."

It took only a moment before the first memory of her son appeared. The image was fuzzy and silent but the woman could see he was about 14 and upset. The woman started to press the green button to lock in the target and then hesitated. The image came into focus and now she could hear the boy's tirades.

"That's so unfair!" Her son's face was crimson and distorted. "I've been planning this for weeks and now you say I can't go!"

"I'm sorry, but you know the rules." It was her voice now and it was disturbing to hear how detached and lifeless it was. "Screaming at me isn't going to change anything."

The boy was lying on the bed with his face buried in a pillow.

"No C's. That was the agreement. No C's and you come home with three of them."

"I never agreed to anything; that was your idea. You never listen to me. You just tell me how it's going to be." "It isn't like," the woman continued the conversation as if she were talking to herself, "you couldn't do better.

You should be making straight A's."

"It doesn't matter. Mom, *please* let me go!"

The woman pressed the green button and the image became fuzzy, the sound muted, and everything faded.

The next memory was from an earlier time. She was on the beach with her son and husband building a sand castle with a red plastic shovel and a bucket of wet sand. The boy was small and wore a bathing suit with pictures of Mickey Mouse. They ran with him, each of them holding a tiny hand, to scoop up sand with the bucket and then raced back to the castle.

The boy screamed in delight. This was the summer before his fifth birthday. They were in Florida at the end of a very hot July and he had never seen the ocean. At first he was frightened of the crashing surf and clung to his dad. The boy's startled face made a small indentation on his father's sunburned chest as they waded into the blue water.

"Daddy no, Daddy no!" he cried when they sat down and let the waves swallow them.

"It's okay," her husband said. "It's only water. Just a giant bathtub filled with water." The little boy laughed.

The woman could smell the salty air, feel the warm sun on her skin, and she wanted to stay in the memory a little longer but she remembered the technician's warning and clicked the button.

She was in her son's bedroom, searching underneath the mattress for mood enhancers. When she found them she sat on the floor and cried.

Click

The three of them were in an elementary class room in front of a large, silver monitor.

"Look, Daddy." Their son stood on his tiptoes and touched a small rectangle on the monitor. The rectangle glowed with a soft, bluish light. "There it is, Daddy!"

"Read it for me, son." He turned and winked at his wife.

In a breathy voice the little boy read:

My daddy is so nice.
He gives me tea on ice.
He sure is the best.
He passes every test,
On that you cannot put any price!

"It's a limerick. Do you like it?"

"I love it. It's wonderful, isn't it, honey?" He turned towards his wife but she had moved to another part of the room.

Click

The woman and her son were standing outside the Cinema Revival Theatre on a cold December afternoon. A light dusting of snow covered the pink granite steps leading to the doors of the lobby. Against a white backdrop, in bold black letters, the movie marquee read:

Heart on a Sleeve

Ninotchka

*Continuous Showings until January 1
Garbo Laughs!*

"Who's Garbo?" the boy asked.

"A movie actress who lived a long time ago."

"Was she funny?"

"Not really, but she was very glamourous."

"Then why does it say she laughs?"

"I don't know. Would you like to see it?"

"Sure, let's go see Garbo laugh."

Her son loved going to the movies. The Cinema Revival Theatre specialized in re-creating film experiences from 150 years ago, before the days of private theatres with 360 degree screens and four dimensional projections. He liked the buttery popcorn, the fizzy carbonated drinks, and the paper tickets for admittance.

Inside the lobby they were greeted by an android dressed as Santa Claus. "Two tickets?"

"Yes, please," the boy answered, although the question was directed to his mother.

The android smiled and handed the tickets to the boy. "The movie's almost over, but it'll start again shortly."

They wandered the luxurious lobby, admiring over-sized paintings of long dead film stars and tossing coins into a marble fountain with a statue of Persephone on top. Except for a few android workers, no one else was there.

"Wow," the boy whispered as if he were in a place of worship, "we're all alone. Isn't that cool?" His face was so open the woman felt an unexpected surge of love for her son and wanted to kiss him, but knew it would only embarrass the boy.

The woman descended deeper into the memory. She was aware the technician stood beside her, still conscious of the metal box in her hand. She wanted to push the button and yet she hesitated once more. Stored away like a favorite sweater in a chest-of-drawers, this memory was a reminder of better times with her son. There was time to stay a little longer before she eradicated it.

At the concession stand the boy asked for popcorn and a box of chocolates. His mother ordered a carbonated drink and they walked into the darkened splendor of the auditorium. A sweeping staircase took them to a double-tiered balcony with mahogany paneling and Tiffany glass. From their seats they could see an empty orchestra pit and a proscenium arch framing the screen. On either side of the screen, murals were painted to look like Pompeian frescoes.

For a while they sat and enjoyed their refreshments in the lush surroundings, sharing the popcorn and chocolates. Soft music played in the orchestra pit until a deep voice behind the screen said: *The film will begin in 10 minutes.*

"I want a drink." The boy dropped the box of popcorn and left his seat to return to the concession stand. The popcorn spilled on the floor and the woman was irritated with him for making a mess. She bent down to pick up the box and the few kernels she saw in the semi-darkness. How stupid of the boy to rush off with only a few minutes left before the start of the movie. He should have gotten his drink earlier. The woman settled into the comfortable seat and tried to relax but the spilt popcorn angered her and she gripped the arms of the seat to steady her nerves. A lovely day was beginning to unravel.

The black ceiling above the balcony was circular with blinking lights that formed the constellations. The woman tried to take her mind off the boy's carelessness by studying the unusual design. To her left were the Big and Little Dippers. On the right was Taurus and in-between were other, unfamiliar ones. When the woman focused on Taurus, it appeared to be spinning and she closed her eyes to stop the sensation of vertigo. From the top of the balcony the woman heard conversation and opened her eyes. She turned around and saw her son silhouetted against the light from a statue niche, talking to a man seated several rows behind them.

The woman's anger over the spilled popcorn was replaced by fear and she called for the boy. He ignored his mother and kept speaking with the man, oblivious to the voice announcing the film would start in 3 minutes. When the woman attempted to leave her seat the dizziness returned and she had to close her eyes again. If she sat quiet and concentrated on the soothing music from the orchestra pit, she would find a way to coax her son back before the movie began.

There was still time to create a perfect memory.

Made in the USA
Charleston, SC
03 February 2017